ELEVATE

MASTERING THE ART OF SALES LEADERSHIP

By Mort Greenberg

———●———————————●———

To every sales manager that gives their best sellers motivation to do more, time to explain how sales works, and guide them each step of the way, this book is for you! To Matt Gilbert and Jim Diaz, thanks for always giving a little extra.

First Paperback edition March 2025

Print Paperback ISBN: 978-1-961059-16-0
Kindle KPF ISBN: 978-1-961059-17-7
Ingram EPUB ISBN: 978-1-961059-18-4

Published by digitalCORE
www.dgtlcore.com

digitalCORE

Other Books by Mort Greenberg

REVENUE VS. SALES SERIES

- **The Singular Focus**
  100+ Tips to Maximize Your Revenue

- **Revenue Boost**
  The Ultimate Sales Plan in Five Steps

- **Straight Up Selling**
  Your Toolbox for Sales Excellence

THE FOCUSED SELLER SERIES

- **Maximizing Human Performance in Sales**
  Unlocking Your Best Results By Thinking
  Like A Business Owner

- **The Sales Tactician**
  Spycraft Techniques for Revenue Success

- **Elevate**
  Mastering the Art of Sales Leadership

- **Beyond The Acquisition**
  Thriving With Private Equity Ownership

CHILDREN'S BOOK SERIES

The Fearless Girl and The Little Guy with Greatness

- **Book 1** - Live Life Motivated
- **Book 2** - Young Leaders Guide
- **Book 3** - Asking Awesome Questions
- **Book 4** - Think to Win
- **Book 5** - Smart Money Moves
- **Book 6** - Wellness Warriors
- **Book 7** - Travel Like a Pro
- **Book 8** - Outdoor Skills

PREFACE

2001 was a pivotal year for the internet, marking both the continued rise of the digital economy and the fallout from the dot-com bubble burst the year prior. 2001 helped create the foundation for the web's future. Google was beginning its rise, broadband was expanding, and the internet was becoming an essential part of daily life. The failures of dot-com startups led to a more sustainable approach to internet business models. The story below brings to life what you will find in the sections and chapters ahead and show how leadership can make a meaningful difference.

At a time of great competition among search engines at this time in 2001, Google, Yahoo!, Excite, AltaVista, Lycos, and Ask Jeeves were still competing. Ask Jeeves was in a unique position. And much of that position was because of people.

Ask Jeeves made its money from advertising, particularly through paid search partnerships. It leveraged keyword-based ads effectively, similar to Google's AdWords model. This model eventually let to an acquisition by InterActiveCorp (IAC) in 2005 for $1.85 billion.

Also in 2001 Matt Gilbert and Jim Diaz had stepped into their roles leading sales at Ask Jeeves. However, this business was struggling to hit its revenue targets.

When Matt and Jim took over, morale was at an all-time low. Their team of twenty salespeople was fractured: some were burned out from chasing unattainable quotas, while others were disengaged, treating the job as a paycheck rather than a career.

Matt and Jim spent their first week observing. They sat in on calls, shadowed meetings, and reviewed the team's performance metrics. It didn't take long to identify the core issues. The team lacked cohesion, the sales processes were outdated, and the compensation plan felt punitive rather than motivational. But most glaringly, the team didn't feel seen or supported.

Determined to turn things around, Matt and Jim called their team together for an open conversation. *"We are not here to tell you what you've done wrong,"* they began. *"We are here to learn from you and help us succeed together. What do you need from us to make that happen?"*

At first, the team was hesitant, but Matt and Jim's sincerity broke through. Over the next hour, they voiced frustrations, shared ideas, and admitted they felt disconnected from the company's vision. Matt and Jim left that meeting with one clear goal: rebuild the team from the ground up.

Matt and Jim's first step was redefining the team's vision. They held a brainstorming session where they crafted a new mission statement: *"To help our clients succeed by delivering tailored solutions."* This shifted the focus from quotas to building long-term customer relationships, which resonated with the team.

Next, Matt and Jim revamped the sales process. They introduced modern CRM tools, the QTC (Quote to Collect) Order Management System, and streamlined workflows to eliminate redundant tasks. They brought in the top training expert and founder of Upstream Group, Doug Weaver, an industry icon in the advertising and media communities. Doug's charge was to teach objection-handling techniques and consultative selling. During one-on-ones, Matt and Jim listened carefully to each rep's struggles and aspirations, offering actionable advice tailored to their unique strengths.

For example, Joey Britton, a high-energy salesperson with a natural gift for doing more and more, was pushing to close many deals at once. However, he overwhelmed himself with volume of activity. Matt and Jim coached him on asking for the sale and listening for buyer signs vs. just asking for information signs. This reduced his activity load and dramatically boosted his close ratio. Within weeks, his booked revenue was up 40%. (Joey went on to have senior sales roles at Yahoo!, Amazon and then became the founder and CEO of SearchMarketers.com)

Meanwhile, Michael Wesner, a reserved but very focused team member, felt overlooked because even though he regularly outperformed his colleagues he was not sure others noticed. Matt and Jim recognized Michael's meticulous attention to detail and placed him in charge of managing larger accounts. Michael thrived in the role, getting large test accounts to commit for much longer terms through consistent, thoughtful follow-ups. These smart follow-ups were a key part in driving renewals and new busines from current customers. (Michael went on to senior roles at several shopping and eCommerce companies and is currently the Chief Commercial Officer at a global hospitality technology company)

To address team cohesion, Matt and Jim organized weekly win-sharing meetings where team members celebrated successes and learned from one another. They also implemented a tiered incentive program, rewarding not just top performers but also those who demonstrated teamwork, creativity, and resilience. This included spot bonuses and the launch of The Presidents Club recognition program.

Gradually, the energy in the salesroom shifted. Reps who once saw each other as competitors now collaborated on strategies. Meetings that used to feel like interrogations became opportunities to share ideas. And as the team gelled, the numbers began to speak for themselves. Within three months, revenue was up 20%, and client satisfaction scores soared.

Six months into their role, Matt and Jim faced a pivotal moment. A major client, worth nearly $1 million annually, threatened to cancel their contract due to unresolved issues with the previous team. Rather than assigning the task to a single rep, Matt and Jim brought the whole team together. They framed the challenge as an opportunity: *"If we save this client, we're proving what we're capable of as a team."*

Together, they crafted a personalized solution for the client, combining Joey's persuasive pitching, Michael's detail-oriented follow-up, and insights from the rest of the team. Not only did they retain the client, but they also expanded the account, adding $500,000 in new revenue.

By the end of Matt and Jim's first year, the new Ask Jeeves had exceeded its sales goals and doubled revenue vs. the previous year. More importantly, the culture had transformed. Reps felt valued and motivated, clients raved about the personalized service, and the once-fragmented team operated like a well-oiled machine.

When Matt and Jim gathered their team to celebrate the year's success, they reflected on their journey. *"This isn't about us,"* they said. *"It's about what we've built together.*

You're not just a sales team—you're a group of leaders, each contributing to something bigger than any one of us."

The applause that followed wasn't just for the numbers—it was for the relationships, the growth, and the belief that Matt and Jim had instilled in their team. Ask Jeeves success wasn't a fluke; it was a testament to what happens when sales managers invest in people.

Matt and Jim didn't just save a struggling team; they built a legacy of trust, empowerment, and excellence. Their story reminds us that the greatest sales leaders don't focus solely on results—they elevate the people around them to achieve greatness together.

INTRODUCTION

Welcome to *"Elevate: Mastering the Art of Sales Leadership,"* the third installment in "The Focused Seller" series. This book is dedicated to transforming sales professionals into exceptional sales leaders, equipped to guide their teams toward unprecedented success.

In the journey through *"The Focused Seller"* series, you began by embedding the mindset of a business owner in *"Maximizing Human Performance In Sales: Unlocking Your Best Results By Thinking Like A Business Owner,"* where we explored essential skills for individual excellence in sales. Then, in *"The Sales Tactician: Spycraft Techniques for Revenue Success,"* you learned how to apply strategic and tactical precision inspired by intelligence operations to your sales approach.

"Elevate" builds on these foundations by focusing on the critical role of leadership in sales. Here, you'll learn how to inspire your team, set visionary goals, and lead with empathy and intelligence. This book will help you craft a cohesive vision, develop high-performing teams, and navigate the complexities of organizational dynamics, thereby ensuring sustained success and growth.

As *"Elevate"* enhances your leadership capabilities, it also prepares you for the subsequent challenges and opportunities described in the final volume, "Beyond The Acquisition: Thriving with Private Equity Ownership." This progression ensures that as you grow in your ability to lead and influence within your organization, you are also equipped to handle the strategic challenges of navigating post-acquisition landscapes and driving success under new ownership structures.

Each book in the series interlinks to provide a comprehensive toolkit for sales excellence at every level—from individual performance and tactical execution to leadership and strategic management. *"Elevate: Mastering the Art of Sales Leadership"* is your step-by-step guide to becoming the kind of leader who not only meets but exceeds all expectations, setting the stage for long-term impact and success.

The pages ahead offer a blueprint for mastering the craft of sales leadership to create your own success story like Matt and Jim who you read about in the preface. This book is designed to equip you with the tools, strategies, and insights needed to elevate your impact—not just on your numbers, but on your team and organization as a whole. Whether you're an aspiring leader looking to step into your first management role or a seasoned professional seeking to refine your approach, this book will challenge and empower you to grow.

Inside, you'll find actionable guidance on every facet of sales leadership, from building high-performing teams and fostering a culture of growth to navigating change and designing strategies that deliver results. Each chapter is packed with practical examples, real-world scenarios, and hands-on exercises to help you apply what you learn. The content isn't just theoretical; it's grounded in the realities of leading sales teams in today's dynamic environment.

This book also addresses the challenges that modern sales leaders face—balancing the art of personal connection with the science of data and technology, motivating teams through uncertainty, and preparing for the future of sales. It provides frameworks for decision-making, tools for communication mastery, and techniques for fostering trust and loyalty among your team members.

What makes this book unique is its focus on holistic leadership. It doesn't stop at tactics and metrics—it gets into the human side of leadership, exploring how to inspire, mentor, and leave a lasting legacy. Leadership is more than a title or a set of skills; it's a commitment to creating value for others and building something that endures. That's the kind of leadership this book hope to help you achieve.

As you turn these pages, you'll be encouraged to think differently, act boldly, and lead with purpose. You'll discover how to align your team with a compelling vision, adapt to shifting market conditions, and build systems that sustain success. Most importantly, you'll learn how to bring out the best in your people while continuously improving yourself.

This is more than a book—it's a toolkit for transformation. Whether you're driving growth, tackling challenges, or preparing for the next stage of your career, the insights within these chapters will guide you toward becoming a more effective, empathetic, and impactful leader.

Get ready to elevate your sales leadership to a new level. Everything you need is right here, waiting for you.

AUTHOR'S NOTE

When I set out to write this book, my goal wasn't just to share strategies or offer advice. It was to create something actionable, meaningful, and personal—something that could serve as a guide for sales leaders navigating the unique challenges of this role. Sales leadership is one of the most dynamic and rewarding positions in any organization, but it's also one of the most complex. It's about much more than hitting quotas or managing a team. It's about inspiring people, adapting to constant change, and creating systems that outlast your tenure.

If you're holding this book, it means you care deeply about your craft. It means you're committed to not only leading your team to success but also growing as a leader yourself. That commitment is rare, and it's what separates good leaders from great ones. This book was written with you in mind—the sales leader who wants to make a difference and build something that truly matters.

As you dive into these pages, you'll find actionable insights on everything from setting a vision that resonates to building high-performing teams, leveraging technology, and navigating the inevitable challenges that come with leadership. You'll learn how to strike the delicate balance between strategy and empathy, data and intuition, results and relationships. And you'll be challenged to think beyond short-term wins, to focus on building a legacy that transforms your team, your organization, and your own career.

This book is also about the human side of leadership. It's about emotional intelligence, communication mastery, and the ability to truly understand and motivate the people you lead. Sales is ultimately about connection—whether it's with your customers or your team.

The best leaders know how to foster trust, inspire loyalty, and create an environment where people can do their best work. The story about Ask Jeeves that you read about in the preface is an important one for me. In addition to Joey and Michael, I also worked for Matt and Jim for many years as one of their sales managers.

You already know that leadership is a journey, not a destination. The best leaders are constantly learning, adapting, and improving. That's why each chapter in this book includes real-world examples and practical exercises to help you put the concepts into action. Whether you're just starting your leadership journey or have decades of experience, I hope this book provides fresh perspectives and inspires you to reach new heights.

Thank you for picking up this book. It's a privilege to share these ideas with you, and I hope they help you elevate your leadership in ways you never imagined possible.

Here's to your success and the incredible impact you will continue to make. Let's get started.

Mort Greenberg

SECTIONS AND CHAPTERS

FOUNDATIONS OF SALES LEADERSHIP

Sales leadership is built on a strong foundation. Without it, even the most ambitious goals and talented teams can falter. This section explores the core principles of sales leadership, from understanding your role as a leader to setting a vision that inspires and aligns your team. You'll learn how to distinguish leadership from management, craft a compelling vision, and build a team that's positioned for long-term success. These chapters provide the essential groundwork you'll need to navigate the complexities of modern sales leadership with confidence.

The Role of a Sales Leader: Understanding Your Impact on the Team and the Business

> *Your influence as a sales leader doesn't just drive results—it defines the culture, direction, and success of your team."*

In the dynamic realm of sales, leadership is not just a position but a pivotal force that can shape the direction, performance, and morale of a sales team. This chapter delves into the multifaceted role of a sales leader, examining how strategic leadership decisions influence both the team's culture and the business's bottom line.

Vision and Strategy

The Cornerstone of Leadership: Setting a Vision

A sales leader's first task is to set a clear, compelling vision for the team. This vision should align with the broader goals of the organization and serve as a guiding light for all sales efforts.

- **Example:** At a leading software company, the sales leader launched a vision-oriented campaign that emphasized the company's commitment to innovation and customer service, significantly enhancing client retention rates.

Strategic Planning and Execution

Effective sales leaders translate vision into action through strategic planning. This involves setting realistic goals, identifying key performance indicators (KPIs), and aligning resources to meet business objectives.

- **Example:** A pharmaceutical sales leader developed a strategy that focused on new market penetration for a recently approved drug, which involved detailed target audience analysis and customized engagement plans for different regions.

Leadership and Team Dynamics

Building and Nurturing a Cohesive Team

A sales leader's ability to assemble and nurture a cohesive team is critical. This includes recruiting the right talent, fostering a supportive environment, and ensuring that team members are continuously learning and developing.

- **Example:** A sales leader at a retail company instituted monthly coaching sessions and team-building activities that not only improved sales skills but also built a stronger, more collaborative team culture.

Motivation and Incentive Structures

Keeping the team motivated is essential for maintaining high levels of energy and commitment. Effective sales leaders create incentive structures that not only reward high performance but also align with the team's values and goals.

- **Example:** At a tech startup, the sales leader implemented a gamified reward system that provided bonuses and extra vacation days to top performers, leading to a 20% increase in sales within the first quarter.

Operational Efficiency

Streamlining Processes for Maximum Efficiency

A sales leader must ensure that all processes are optimized to support the team's efforts. This includes leveraging technology to automate tasks and free up time for high-value activities.

- **Example:** A sales leader introduced a new CRM system that automated lead tracking and follow-ups, which reduced the time salespeople spent on administrative tasks by 40%.

Data-Driven Decision Making

In today's digital age, being able to interpret and act on data is crucial. Sales leaders should be adept at using data to make informed decisions that drive the team forward.

■ **Example:** By analyzing sales trends and customer feedback, a sales leader identified a need for a new product feature, which once implemented, significantly boosted sales and customer satisfaction.

Impacting the Business

Driving Revenue Growth

The ultimate goal of any sales leader is to drive revenue growth. This is achieved not only through direct sales efforts but also by improving the efficiency and effectiveness of the sales process.

■ **Example:** A sales leader restructured the sales funnel to focus more on high-value prospects, which increased the conversion rate by 15% and significantly raised overall revenues.

Enhancing Customer Relationships

Strong customer relationships are the backbone of successful sales. A sales leader plays a crucial role in developing strategies for customer engagement and retention.

■ **Example:** By implementing a customer loyalty program, a sales leader managed to increase repeat customer rates by 25% over two years.

Workshop Activities

Activity 1: Vision Crafting Workshop

Participants are divided into groups and tasked with developing a vision statement for a new sales initiative. They will present their vision to the group, along with strategic steps they would take to realize this vision.

Activity 2: Strategic Sales Planning Game

Teams will participate in a competitive simulation game where they must design and execute a sales strategy for a fictional product. They will analyze market data, set sales targets, and choose strategic actions to outperform the other teams.

Activity 3: Leadership Role-Play

Participants will engage in role-play scenarios that challenge them to handle difficult leadership situations, such as motivating a demotivated team member, managing conflict within the team, and communicating changes in strategy.

Conclusion

Understanding the comprehensive role of a sales leader is essential for anyone aspiring to lead a team to success. From setting a vision to operationalizing strategies, and from nurturing team dynamics to making data-driven decisions, a sales leader's responsibilities are crucial in shaping the team's achievements and, by extension, the company's success. This chapter has laid out foundational strategies and practical examples to guide new and seasoned leaders alike in mastering the art of sales leadership.

Leadership vs. Management: Identifying the Differences and When to Apply Each Skill

"

A manager keeps the wheels turning; a leader inspires the team to dream bigger and achieve more.

"

Understanding the distinction between leadership and management is crucial for anyone in a sales leadership role. While these terms are often used interchangeably, they embody different skills, responsibilities, and approaches to achieving organizational goals. This chapter explores these differences and guides readers on when and how to apply each skill effectively.

Defining Leadership and Management

Leadership: Inspiring and Influencing

Leadership involves setting a vision, inspiring people to believe in that vision, and motivating them to achieve collective goals. Leaders focus on influencing team culture and values, often looking at the big picture and thinking strategically about the future.

Example: A sales leader might inspire the team by sharing a compelling vision for dominating a new market segment, emphasizing the impact of each team member's role in this journey.

Management: Planning and Organizing

In contrast, management focuses more on administering and making sure that the day-to-day operations are aligned with the company's standards and goals. Managers are often tasked with planning, organizing, and monitoring progress to ensure efficiency and effectiveness in achieving specific objectives.

Example: A sales manager may implement a CRM system to better track client interactions and ensure that the sales process is efficient and meets organizational standards.

When to Lead and
When to Manage

Leading During Change

Leadership skills are particularly important during times of significant change or uncertainty when teams need vision and inspiration. Leaders guide their teams through transformation by providing a clear sense of direction and purpose.

Example: When a company decides to pivot its product line in response to competitive pressures, a sales leader will help the team understand the reasons for the change and get them excited about the new opportunities.

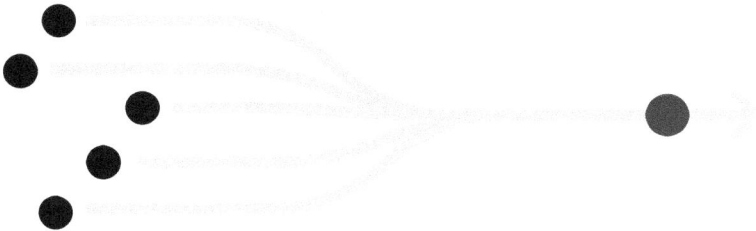

Managing to Maintain Stability

Management skills come to the forefront when the focus is on stability, consistency, and optimization of processes. This is crucial for ensuring that established systems function smoothly and efficiently.

Example: In the aftermath of a successful product launch, a sales manager might focus on fine-tuning follow-up processes and ensuring the team meets service standards during the implementation phase.

Integrating Leadership and Management

Balancing Both for Success

The most effective sales leaders know how to balance leadership and management skills. They provide vision while also ensuring that the day-to-day operations support this vision.

Example: A sales leader might set ambitious annual goals (leadership) and break them down into quarterly targets (management) that are regularly reviewed and adjusted as needed.

Workshop Activities

Activity 1: Role Play

Participants are divided into groups and given scenarios that require either a leadership or management approach, such as handling a team resistant to new sales techniques (leadership) or organizing a sales conference (management). Each group discusses and role-plays how they would handle the situation.

Activity 2: Leadership vs. Management Assessment

Individuals complete a self-assessment to identify their strengths and weaknesses in leadership and management skills. Results are discussed in small groups to find ways to develop weaker areas.

Activity 3: Vision Mapping

In this activity, participants develop a vision for a hypothetical sales campaign and then create a detailed plan to implement this vision. The exercise emphasizes the integration of leadership vision with practical management steps.

Conclusion

Recognizing when to lead and when to manage is vital for sales leaders. By understanding the nuances between these roles, sales leaders can more effectively inspire their teams and ensure operational success, leading to sustained growth and achievement in competitive markets. This chapter has provided frameworks and practical examples to help readers develop both sets of skills, supported by interactive activities designed to reinforce learning and application in real-world scenarios.

CHAPTER 3

Setting the Vision: Crafting and Communicating a Compelling Sales Vision

"

A compelling vision is the North Star that aligns your team's efforts and inspires them to surpass expectations.

"

A clear and compelling vision is foundational for guiding a sales team to success. It provides direction, motivates team members, and aligns efforts toward common goals. This chapter explores how to craft and effectively communicate a sales vision that resonates and drives performance.

The Importance of a Vision in Sales

Why Vision Matters

In the fast-paced, target-driven world of sales, a strong vision serves as a north star, helping the team navigate challenges and stay focused on long-term objectives. It articulates what the team strives to achieve and why their work matters.

Example: A technology company's sales leader crafts a vision centered on revolutionizing how businesses interact with their customers through advanced AI solutions, aiming to capture and lead the market by delivering exceptional value.

Crafting the Vision

Identifying Core Values and Objectives

The first step in crafting a vision is to clearly define the core values and objectives that your team or company holds. This involves deep reflection on what sets your business apart and how you can make a difference in the market.

Example: The sales leader at a healthcare solutions company might focus on the core value of improving patient care through innovation, shaping a vision that emphasizes making advanced medical technologies accessible to healthcare providers.

Envisioning Future Success

Imagining the future success of the team helps in shaping a vision that is both aspirational and achievable. It should challenge the team but also remain grounded in reality.

Example: A sales leader envisions tripling the market share over the next five years by aligning sales strategies with evolving consumer preferences and emerging market trends.

Communicating the Vision

Clarity and Consistency

A vision must be communicated clearly and consistently across all levels of the team. It should be simple enough to be remembered and powerful enough to inspire.

Example: During team meetings, the sales leader consistently reiterates the vision using a concise message: *"Empower every retailer to thrive in the digital age."*

Incorporating Storytelling

Using storytelling to convey the vision can make it more relatable and engaging. Share stories of potential impacts, customer successes, or a future state where the team's efforts have made a significant difference.

Example: The leader shares a story about a small retailer who transformed their business using the company's solutions, exemplifying the vision's impact.

Living the Vision

Leading by Example

Leaders must embody the vision themselves. By demonstrating commitment through actions, leaders can encourage their team to internalize and pursue the vision enthusiastically.

- **Example:** A sales leader actively engages in key sales initiatives that align with the vision, showing dedication and setting a behavioral standard for the team.

Aligning Resources and Strategies

Ensure that all resources, strategies, and operations are aligned with the vision. This may involve training programs, sales strategies, and internal processes that reinforce the vision's objectives.

- **Example:** Implementing a training program that emphasizes consultative selling, which is critical to realizing the vision of becoming trusted advisors to customers.

Workshop Activities

Activity 1: Vision Crafting Workshop

Participants are tasked with creating a vision statement for a new product or market the company is planning to enter. They use market data, customer insights, and company values to craft a vision that is both inspiring and strategic.

Activity 2: Vision Communication Role-Play

In this activity, each participant practices communicating the vision to different audiences, such as new hires, potential investors, and non-sales employees, adjusting their messaging to suit audience understanding and interests.

Activity 3: Vision Alignment Audit

Groups review current sales strategies and resources to identify areas that are not aligned with the company's vision. They propose adjustments and develop an action plan to enhance alignment.

Conclusion

Setting and communicating a compelling sales vision is a dynamic and ongoing process that requires thoughtful development and consistent reinforcement. By effectively crafting and living out a vision, sales leaders can inspire their teams to achieve remarkable results and sustain long-term success in competitive markets. This chapter provides practical tools and exercises to help leaders successfully implement these concepts.

CHAPTER 4

Building Your Team: Hiring the Right People and Positioning Them for Success

> *The right people, in the right roles, with the right support, are the foundation of any high-performing sales team.*

A sales leader's ability to build a strong team is pivotal to the success of any organization. This chapter outlines strategies for recruiting the right individuals and effectively positioning them to achieve both personal and organizational goals.

Understanding Team Needs

Assessing Skills and Gaps

Before beginning the recruitment process, it's crucial to assess the current team's composition – identifying skill gaps and understanding the types of personalities that would enhance team dynamics.

Example: A sales leader at a SaaS company conducts skills assessments to identify gaps in technical selling and customer relationship management, highlighting the need for recruits who excel in these areas.

Recruiting the Right Talent

Defining Ideal Candidate Profiles

Craft detailed profiles for ideal candidates that align with both the company's sales goals and cultural values. This should include necessary skills, desired experiences, and personality traits that fit the team's dynamics.

Example: For a luxury car dealership, the ideal candidate profile might emphasize not only sales experience but also a passion for automotive technology and a charismatic presence.

Effective Interviewing Techniques

Implement interviewing techniques that allow you to assess both skill proficiency and cultural fit. Behavioral interview questions can reveal how candidates have handled past situations and whether their approach aligns with your team's values.

■ **Example:** Asking candidates to describe a time they overcame a significant sales challenge can provide insights into their resilience and problem-solving skills.

Onboarding and Training

Structured Onboarding Process

A well-structured onboarding process is essential for integrating new hires into the team, making them feel valued, and speeding up their time to productivity.

■ **Example:** A tech company uses a 90-day onboarding plan that includes product training, shadowing top performers, and initial goal-setting sessions to ensure new salespeople understand their roles and the company's expectations.

Continuous Training and Development

Invest in continuous training and development to keep the team's skills sharp and up-to-date. This not only helps in achieving sales targets but also aids in employee retention by showing a commitment to their growth.

■ **Example:** An annual retreat focused on advanced sales techniques and emerging industry trends keeps the team engaged and informed.

Positioning for Success

Aligning Roles with Skills and Aspirations

Ensure that roles and responsibilities are aligned with individual skills and career aspirations. This alignment increases job satisfaction and effectiveness.

Example: Recognizing a team member's proficiency in and passion for client relationship management, a sales leader might shift their focus from new client acquisition to key account management.

Performance Management and Feedback

Establish a transparent performance management system that includes regular feedback and reviews. This helps individuals understand how they are contributing to the team's goals and where they can improve.

Example: Monthly one-on-one meetings to discuss achievements, challenges, and personal development plans ensure that team members feel supported and guided.

Workshop Activities

Activity 1: Role-Playing Recruitment

Participants role-play different stages of the recruitment process, from interviewing to evaluating candidates, to better understand effective techniques for assessing skills and cultural fit.

Activity 2: Onboarding Design Challenge

Teams work together to design an onboarding program for new sales hires. They must consider elements that ensure a fast and effective integration into the team.

Activity 3: Skills Mapping Workshop

Each team member maps out their current skills and career aspirations. The group then discusses how to align these with the team's needs and individual development paths.

Conclusion

Building a high-performing sales team involves careful planning from recruitment to ongoing development. By hiring the right people and positioning them for success, sales leaders can create a robust team capable of meeting and exceeding business objectives. This chapter has provided practical guidelines and activities to help sales leaders effectively build and nurture their teams.

DEVELOPING YOUR LEADERSHIP SKILLS

Great leaders are not born—they're built through continuous growth and refinement. In this section, we'll dive into the personal and interpersonal skills that separate good sales leaders from great ones. From emotional intelligence and communication mastery to decision-making and conflict resolution, you'll discover practical strategies for honing your leadership style. These chapters will challenge you to lead with empathy, clarity, and decisiveness, empowering your team to excel while fostering trust and collaboration.

CHAPTER 5

Emotional Intelligence: Harnessing EQ to Lead and Inspire Your Team

" "

Empathy and self-awareness are as essential as strategy in leading and inspiring your team.

Emotional intelligence (EQ) is a critical component of effective leadership, especially in the high-stakes world of sales. This chapter explores how sales leaders can develop and use EQ to enhance their leadership abilities, foster a positive team environment, and drive performance.

The Components of
Emotional Intelligence

Understanding EQ

Emotional intelligence involves the ability to understand, use, and manage your own emotions in positive ways to relieve stress, communicate effectively, empathize with others, overcome challenges, and defuse conflict. EQ can be broken down into five key components: self-awareness, self-regulation, motivation, empathy, and social skills.

Example: A sales leader with high self-awareness recognizes their stress triggers and actively works to mitigate these before they impact team interactions and decision-making.

Developing Self-Awareness
and Self-Regulation

Cultivating Self-Awareness

Self-awareness is knowing one's emotions, strengths, weaknesses, drives, values, and goals—and their impact on others. Leaders with high self-awareness are often more effective and get more respect.

Example: A leader notices they feel impatient during team updates and uses this awareness to adjust their behavior, ensuring they listen more attentively.

Enhancing Self-Regulation

Leaders who regulate themselves effectively rarely verbally attack others, make rushed or emotional decisions, stereotype people, or compromise their values. Self-regulation is about staying in control.

■ **Example:** When a sales deal goes awry, instead of showing frustration, a sales leader calmly assesses the situation, showing the team how to handle disappointment professionally.

Leveraging Motivation and Empathy

Fostering Motivation

Highly motivated leaders work consistently toward their goals, love a challenge, and have extremely high standards for the quality of their work. They use this drive to motivate their teams by setting and exemplifying high performance standards.

■ **Example:** A sales leader sets challenging yet achievable goals for the team, encouraging them through positive reinforcement and recognition of their efforts.

Practicing Empathy

Empathy is crucial for managing a successful team or organization. It allows leaders to understand the emotional makeup of their people and treat them according to their emotional reactions.

- **Example:** Recognizing that one of their team members is struggling with personal issues, a considerate sales leader might offer them flexible working arrangements or additional support.

Enhancing Social Skills

Building and Maintaining Relationships

Effective social skills in leadership translate into the ability to manage relationships and build networks, and an adeptness at finding common ground and building rapport.

- **Example:** A sales leader uses their social skills to facilitate a networking event, where they encourage their team to connect with potential clients and industry peers.

Workshop Activities

Activity 1: EQ Self-Assessment

Participants complete a self-assessment to identify their EQ strengths and areas for improvement. This helps them understand how well they perceive, control, and evaluate emotions.

Activity 2: Role-Playing Emotional Responses

In this activity, participants role-play various scenarios to practice responses that demonstrate high EQ, such as dealing with a team conflict, handling stressful situations, or motivating a demotivated team member.

Activity 3: Empathy Circle

Participants engage in an "empathy circle," where they share personal experiences and practice empathy by listening actively and responding appropriately. This helps enhance understanding and support within the team.

Conclusion

Harnessing emotional intelligence is essential for sales leaders who aim to lead effectively and inspire their teams. By developing skills like self-awareness, empathy, and social adeptness, leaders can create a more conducive work environment that promotes higher sales performance and job satisfaction. This chapter has provided a nuanced analysis along with practical examples and workshop activities to help leaders improve their EQ skills in real-world settings.

CHAPTER 6

Communication Mastery: Effective Communication Strategies for Sales Leaders

"

Effective communication isn't just about what you say—it's about how well your team understands, connects, and acts.

"

Effective communication is the cornerstone of successful leadership in any field, especially in sales where clarity and persuasion are paramount. This chapter delves into the nuances of effective communication strategies tailored for sales leaders, providing tools and examples to enhance interaction with teams and clients.

Understanding Communication in Sales Leadership

The Importance of Communication

Effective communication helps to ensure that team members understand their roles, the goals of the organization, and how their actions align with broader business objectives. For sales leaders, being an effective communicator also means being able to inspire and motivate the team, handle objections, and forge strong relationships.

Example: A sales leader communicates the quarterly targets during a team meeting with clear explanations of each member's role in achieving these targets, using visual aids and interactive elements to ensure understanding and engagement.

Strategies for Effective Communication

Adapting Communication Styles

Different situations and audiences require different communication styles. Sales leaders must adapt their approach whether they are speaking to the board, addressing their team, or dealing with customers.

Example: When addressing the board, a sales leader might use formal language and data-driven insights, whereas team pep talks might be more informal and motivational, using storytelling to connect and inspire.

Active Listening

Active listening involves fully concentrating, understanding, responding, and then remembering what is being said. This is crucial not only for building rapport but also for accurately assessing and responding to the needs of the team and clients.

- **Example:** During one-on-one sessions, a sales leader practices active listening by summarizing what the team member has said and asking questions to clarify their needs and concerns.

Feedback Mechanisms

Implementing effective feedback mechanisms is essential for maintaining open channels of communication and continuous improvement. Feedback should be timely, constructive, and specific.

- **Example:** After a sales pitch, a leader provides specific feedback to the team member, highlighting what was done well and giving concrete suggestions for improvement based on observed performance.

Handling Difficult Conversations

Navigating Conflict

Conflicts are inevitable in any team. Handling them with tact and effective communication can prevent them from escalating and can even turn them into opportunities for growth and improvement.

Example: When a dispute arises between two team members over sales territories, the sales leader mediates the situation by facilitating a discussion where each party shares their perspective, working towards a mutually beneficial resolution.

Delivering Tough Messages

Sometimes leaders need to convey decisions that are unpopular or disappointing. How these messages are delivered can impact team morale and respect for leadership.

Example: When budget cuts require scaling back team bonuses, the sales leader explains the reasons transparently, discusses how the decision was made, and explores alternative ways to motivate and reward the team.

Workshop Activities

Activity 1: Communication Style Role-Play

Participants role-play various scenarios requiring different communication styles (e.g., delivering a sales strategy to executives vs. coaching a sales rep). This helps participants understand how to adjust their communication based on their audience and context.

Activity 2: Active Listening Exercises

Participants pair up to practice active listening. One partner shares a work-related issue while the other practices listening attentively, asks clarifying questions, and provides feedback, which is then critiqued by the group.

Activity 3: Handling Difficult Conversations

Participants are given scenarios of difficult conversations (e.g., addressing underperformance, handling objections from customers) and role-play these situations. Peers and facilitators provide feedback on the communication strategies used.

Conclusion

Mastering communication is vital for sales leaders to effectively lead their teams, manage conflicts, and maintain a positive work environment. The strategies discussed in this chapter, along with real-world examples and practical exercises, equip sales leaders with the skills needed to excel in all facets of communication. These skills will ensure that they not only convey their messages effectively but also foster an atmosphere of openness and mutual respect.

Decision Making: Techniques for Making Quick and Effective Decisions Under Pressure

"

Great leaders make tough decisions quickly and confidently, balancing logic with intuition.

"

The ability to make quick, effective decisions under pressure is a defining trait of successful sales leaders. This chapter explores decision-making techniques that enhance both speed and accuracy, helping leaders manage the dynamic and often high-stakes environment of sales.

Understanding the Dynamics of Decision-Making

The Complexity of Sales Decisions

Sales leaders often face decisions that have significant financial implications and affect team morale. Understanding the types of decisions (strategic, tactical, operational) and their impacts can help leaders prioritize and apply the appropriate decision-making technique.

Example: A sales leader faces a strategic decision about entering a new market. This decision requires thorough analysis and could significantly affect the company's long-term growth.

Decision-Making Models

The OODA Loop (Observe, Orient, Decide, Act)

Developed by military strategist John Boyd, the OODA loop emphasizes rapid observation and decision-making. It's particularly useful in sales when conditions change rapidly, and data must be quickly assessed.

Example: During a competitive bid, a sales leader uses the OODA loop to quickly adjust their proposal in response to last-minute information about a competitor's offer.

Cost-Benefit Analysis (CBA)

Cost-Benefit Analysis involves weighing the costs and benefits of a decision to determine the best course of action. It's useful for decisions that are not urgent but have significant impact.

Example: Before investing in a new sales automation tool, a sales leader conducts a CBA to evaluate the expected improvements in efficiency against the cost of the software and training.

Techniques for Enhancing Decision Quality

Reducing Cognitive Biases

Cognitive biases can severely impair decision-making. Techniques like seeking second opinions, considering the opposite course of action, and setting pre-determined criteria can help mitigate biases.

Example: To avoid confirmation bias when deciding on a marketing strategy, a sales leader solicits opinions from various team members, including skeptics of the strategy.

Scenario Planning

This technique involves envisioning various future scenarios and planning responses in advance. It prepares leaders to make decisions quickly by considering multiple possibilities before they unfold.

> **Example:** A sales leader uses scenario planning for key account negotiations, preparing for best-case, worst-case, and most likely scenarios regarding client demands and competitive actions.

Developing Decision-Making Speed

Practice Under Pressure

Regularly putting oneself in low-stake situations that simulate pressure helps improve the ability to make decisions quickly when real high-stake situations arise.

> **Example:** A sales leader practices making quick decisions during team simulations that mimic tight-deadline scenarios.

Timeboxing Decisions

Setting a strict time limit for making a decision can prevent overthinking and speed up the decision-making process.

> **Example:** When deciding on weekly priorities, a sales leader allocates 30 minutes every Monday morning to set the week's agenda and stick to it.

Workshop Activities

Activity 1: OODA Loop Simulation

Participants engage in a fast-paced simulation that requires using the OODA loop. They observe a rapidly changing sales scenario, orient themselves to the implications, decide on a course of action, and act, all within a timed framework.

Activity 2: Cost-Benefit Analysis Role Play

Teams are given a business decision to make, such as whether to hire more staff or increase marketing spend. They must perform a cost-benefit analysis and present their findings and decision to the group.

Activity 3: Bias Identification Workshop

This activity involves participants reviewing past decisions they have made, identifying possible cognitive biases, and discussing how these could have been mitigated.

Conclusion

Effective decision-making under pressure is crucial for sales leaders, who must balance speed with accuracy to drive performance and achieve strategic goals. The techniques and models explored in this chapter provide leaders with tools to enhance their decision-making capabilities. Through practice and the application of these strategies, sales leaders can become more adept at navigating the complexities of their roles.

CHAPTER 8

Conflict Resolution: Handling Disputes and Maintaining Team Harmony

"

Resolving conflict isn't about winning—it's about restoring harmony and strengthening team dynamics.

"

Conflict is a natural part of any team dynamic, particularly in high-pressure environments like sales. Effectively managing and resolving conflicts is crucial for maintaining team harmony and ensuring sustained productivity. This chapter explores strategies for conflict resolution tailored for sales leaders, backed by practical examples and engaging workshop activities.

Understanding
Conflict in Sales Teams

Types of Conflicts

Conflicts in sales teams can arise from various sources including competition for resources, miscommunications, personality clashes, and differences in value or goal alignment. Recognizing the type of conflict is the first step in addressing it effectively.

■ **Example:** Two sales team members argue over the allocation of leads from a high-value region, each claiming they can better convert prospects into customers.

The Impact of Unresolved Conflict

Unresolved conflicts can lead to decreased morale, reduced productivity, and even the loss of valuable employees. Effective conflict resolution not only addresses the immediate disagreement but also strengthens the team by improving communication and understanding.

■ **Example:** Ongoing disputes about sales territories lead to a toxic work environment, resulting in several team members requesting transfers or leaving the company.

Conflict Resolution Strategies

Active Listening and Effective Communication

Encouraging open communication and practicing active listening are key to understanding the root causes of conflict and finding a mutually acceptable solution.

Example: During a conflict resolution meeting, a sales leader listens attentively to each party's concerns and summarizes their points to ensure all voices are heard and understood.

Mediation and Facilitation

Sometimes, a neutral third party can help facilitate a resolution by mediating the discussion. This can be particularly effective when conflicts are entrenched or the parties involved are highly emotional.

Example: A senior leader or HR specialist steps in to mediate a heated argument between sales team members over account distribution.

Creating Win-Win Situations

Finding solutions that benefit all parties involved can help resolve conflicts amicably. This approach focuses on collaboration rather than competition.

Example: To resolve a conflict over lead distribution, a sales leader creates a rotation system that allows team members to take turns handling high-value leads, ensuring everyone gets equal opportunities.

Maintaining Team Harmony

Establishing Clear Rules and Expectations

Setting clear rules and expectations about behavior and handling disputes can prevent conflicts from arising and ensure they are managed effectively when they do occur.

Example: A sales team has a clear policy on lead handling and dispute resolution, which is reviewed and agreed upon by all team members during onboarding.

Regular Team-Building Activities

Engaging in regular team-building activities can strengthen relationships and improve communication among team members, making it easier to handle conflicts when they arise.

Example: A sales team participates in monthly team-building exercises that focus on communication skills, trust-building, and collaborative problem-solving.

Workshop Activities

Activity 1: Role-Playing Conflict Scenarios

Participants role-play different conflict scenarios relevant to sales environments. This helps them practice negotiation and mediation skills in a controlled setting.

Activity 2: Active Listening Exercise

Participants pair up to practice active listening techniques. One person discusses an issue they've faced, while the other practices listening without interrupting, then repeats back what they heard to ensure understanding.

Activity 3: Creating a Conflict Resolution Plan

Teams work together to create a conflict resolution plan for their team, including preventive measures and steps to take when conflicts arise. This plan is then presented to the group for feedback.

Conclusion

Conflict resolution is an essential skill for sales leaders, necessary for maintaining a productive and harmonious team. By employing effective communication strategies, mediation techniques, and proactive team-building activities, leaders can manage conflicts effectively and foster a positive team environment. This chapter provides the tools and knowledge needed to navigate these challenges, supported by practical examples and interactive activities.

SALES STRATEGY AND EXECUTION

Leadership without strategy is like a ship without a compass. In this section, we shift our focus to the tactical side of sales leadership—designing strategies that drive results and adapting to ever-changing market conditions. You'll learn how to analyze markets, streamline processes, and leverage technology to enhance performance. These chapters will provide the tools you need to align your team's efforts with organizational goals and execute strategies that deliver measurable outcomes.

CHAPTER 9

Designing Sales Strategies: Creating Plans That Deliver Results

> *A strong sales strategy turns vision into action and action into results.*

A well-crafted sales strategy is essential for driving business growth and achieving competitive advantage. This chapter explores the critical components of designing effective sales strategies that align with company goals, market conditions, and customer needs, featuring in-depth analysis, practical examples, and interactive workshop activities.

Understanding the Components of a Sales Strategy

Market Analysis

Before designing a sales strategy, a thorough analysis of the market is crucial. This includes understanding the competitive landscape, identifying customer segments, and recognizing emerging trends that may impact sales.

Example: A sales leader at a software company conducts a detailed market analysis that reveals a growing demand for cloud-based solutions among small businesses, guiding the strategic focus towards this segment.

Goal Setting

Effective sales strategies are anchored in clear, measurable goals. These goals should be ambitious yet achievable and aligned with broader business objectives.

Example: The goal for a new health supplement product line might be to capture 10% of the market share within the first year by focusing on health-conscious consumers aged 25-40.

Developing Sales Tactics

Segmentation and Targeting

Once the market has been analyzed and goals set, the next step is to segment the market and identify target demographics. Strategies are then tailored to these specific groups to maximize impact.

Example: For high-end cosmetic products, a sales strategy might target professional women in urban areas with disposable income, using premium pricing and luxury branding.

Channel Optimization

Choosing the right channels to reach customers is critical. This may involve a mix of online and offline sales platforms, depending on where the target customers are most likely to be engaged.

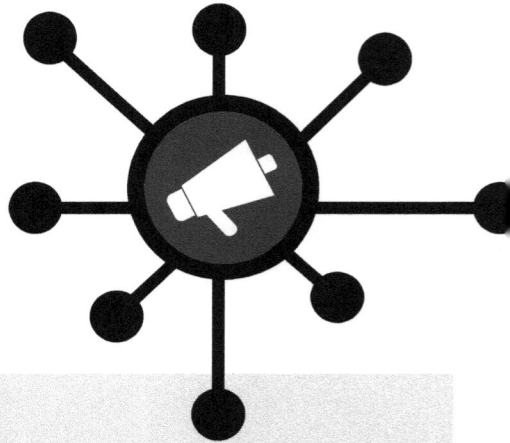

Example: A consumer electronics company uses a combination of e-commerce platforms and retail partnerships to reach a broader audience.

Sales Enablement

Providing the sales team with the right tools, information, and resources to effectively sell the product is essential. This includes training, sales collateral, and access to customer relationship management (CRM) systems.

Example: A B2B company implements a new CRM system that includes features for tracking customer interactions and automates follow-up tasks, significantly improving lead management.

Implementing the Strategy

Execution Plan

A detailed execution plan is vital, outlining who does what, when, and how. Regular checkpoints and adjustments ensure the strategy remains effective and agile in response to market changes.

■ **Example:** The launch of a new fitness tracker includes a phased rollout plan, starting with influencers and early adopters in key metropolitan areas, followed by a broader national marketing campaign.

Monitoring and Adjusting

Continuous monitoring of the sales strategy's performance against set goals is necessary. This allows for timely adjustments in response to feedback and changing conditions.

■ **Example:** Monthly sales reviews reveal that an expected uptick in product adoption is lagging; the strategy is quickly adjusted to increase promotional activities and customer incentives.

Workshop Activities

Activity 1: Market Analysis Simulation

Participants engage in a simulated market analysis exercise where they gather and analyze data on a fictional market, identifying key trends and competitive dynamics.

Activity 2: Strategy Design Workshop

Teams work together to design a sales strategy for a new product. They define goals, choose target segments, select sales channels, and plan the enablement resources needed.

Activity 3: Role-Playing Execution Challenges

Participants role-play various scenarios that might arise during the execution of a sales strategy, such as handling a competitor's unexpected product launch or dealing with supply chain disruptions. This helps them think on their feet and adapt strategies under pressure.

Conclusion

Designing and implementing an effective sales strategy requires a deep understanding of the market, clear goal setting, strategic resource allocation, and agile execution. By following the principles outlined in this chapter, sales leaders can create robust strategies that not only meet but exceed their sales targets, driving meaningful business growth. This chapter provides the framework and tools necessary to achieve these outcomes, enriched with real-world examples and engaging workshop activities to enhance learning and application.

CHAPTER 10

Market Analysis and Adaptation: Understanding and Reacting to Market Dynamics

"

Success in sales depends on your ability to read the market and adjust your approach with agility.

"

Effective sales strategies hinge on a deep understanding of market dynamics and the ability to adapt swiftly to these changes. This chapter explores the essential processes of conducting thorough market analyses and adapting sales strategies accordingly, ensuring that sales leaders can anticipate shifts and maintain competitive advantage.

Understanding Market Dynamics

Fundamentals of Market Analysis

Market analysis involves examining various elements such as market size, growth rate, trends, customer demographics, and competitor activities. This foundational knowledge helps sales leaders make informed decisions and predict future changes.

Example: A sales leader at an automotive company conducts a market analysis that reveals an increasing demand for electric vehicles among urban consumers aged 25-40. This insight leads to a strategic shift towards this market segment.

Utilizing Data-Driven Insights

Modern sales strategies are bolstered by data-driven insights gathered from customer data, industry reports, and competitive analysis. Leveraging this data effectively allows sales leaders to identify new opportunities and anticipate potential challenges.

Example: By analyzing sales data and customer feedback, a sales leader at a software company identifies a significant demand for cloud storage solutions among small businesses, prompting a realignment of the sales focus.

Adapting to Market Changes

Strategic Flexibility

The ability to adapt to market changes is crucial for sustaining business growth. Sales leaders need to develop flexible strategies that can be adjusted as market conditions evolve.

- **Example:** When a new competitor enters the market with a disruptive technology, a sales leader quickly reevaluates their product offerings and adjusts their sales pitch to highlight unique features not offered by the competitor.

Implementing Adaptive Sales Strategies

Adaptive sales strategies might involve changes in pricing, promotions, product offerings, or sales channels based on ongoing market analysis.

- **Example:** During an economic downturn, a sales leader implements a flexible pricing strategy that maintains sales volume and customer loyalty until market conditions improve.

Ensuring Continuous
Learning and Improvement

Learning from Success and Failure

Continuous learning from both successes and failures helps sales teams evolve and stay competitive. Regular reviews of sales performance against market expectations are essential.

- **Example:** After a less successful product launch, a sales leader conducts a post-mortem analysis to understand what went wrong and how to avoid similar pitfalls in future strategies.

Feedback Loops and Market Research

Establishing systematic feedback loops with customers, and conducting ongoing market research helps sales leaders stay ahead of trends and customer preferences.

Example: A consumer electronics company regularly gathers customer feedback through surveys and focus groups to gauge responses to their new product features.

Workshop Activities

Activity 1: Simulating Market Shifts

Participants engage in a simulation game where they must respond to unexpected market shifts, such as new regulations or sudden changes in consumer behavior. Teams will need to analyze the situation and make strategic adjustments on the fly.

Activity 2: Developing a Market Analysis Framework

Teams collaborate to develop a comprehensive market analysis framework that includes key metrics and sources of information they will monitor regularly. This framework helps ensure that they are consistently aware of the market dynamics.

Activity 3: Role-Playing Adaptation Strategies

Participants role-play various scenarios where they must adapt their sales strategy based on hypothetical market changes. This activity encourages creative thinking and flexibility in decision-making.

Conclusion

Understanding and reacting to market dynamics are critical skills for sales leaders. This chapter provides a thorough exploration of the techniques for conducting effective market analyses and adapting strategies to meet changing conditions. By employing these practices, sales leaders can ensure their teams are agile, responsive, and continuously aligned with market realities.

CHAPTER 11

Operational Efficiency: Streamlining Processes for Maximum Productivity

"

Streamlined processes are the backbone of productivity and consistent performance.

"

Operational efficiency is paramount in sales, where the speed and effectiveness of processes can significantly impact both top-line growth and bottom-line profitability. This chapter delves into strategies for streamlining sales processes, enhancing productivity, and reducing waste, ensuring that sales teams operate at their peak performance.

Understanding
Operational Efficiency

Importance of Efficient Operations

Efficient operations enable sales teams to respond more quickly to opportunities, reduce costs, and improve customer satisfaction. Streamlining processes ensures that resources are utilized effectively, and team members are focused on high-value activities.

■ **Example:** A software sales team automates routine follow-up emails, allowing sales representatives to spend more time engaging in personalized customer interactions that are more likely to close deals.

Identifying Inefficiencies

The first step to improving operational efficiency is identifying bottlenecks and redundancies in the sales process. This might involve analyzing workflow, communication channels, and resource allocation.

■ **Example:** Upon reviewing the sales pipeline, a sales leader identifies that deals are consistently stalling at the proposal stage, prompting a review and simplification of the proposal approval process.

Techniques for Enhancing Efficiency

Process Automation

Automation tools can handle repetitive tasks, such as data entry, lead scoring, and initial customer inquiries, freeing up sales staff to focus on closing deals and building customer relationships.

■ **Example:** A B2B company implements a CRM system that automatically updates lead scores based on interaction data, ensuring that sales efforts are focused on the most promising leads.

Lean Sales Processes

Adopting lean principles in sales involves continuously looking for ways to eliminate waste and ensure that every step in the sales process adds value to the customer.

■ **Example:** A sales leader restructures the team's reporting system to require only essential metrics, significantly reducing the time spent on compiling and analyzing reports.

Continuous Training and Development

Regular training ensures that sales teams are proficient in the latest sales technologies and methodologies, which can enhance productivity and effectiveness.

■ **Example:** Monthly training sessions introduce sales staff to new features in their sales software and best practices for leveraging technology to streamline their workflow.

Implementing and Sustaining Changes

Pilot Testing Changes

Before rolling out process changes across the entire sales team, pilot testing with a small group can help identify potential issues and ensure that the new processes achieve the desired improvement.

Example: A pilot test of a new lead qualification process in one sales region helps refine the criteria before the new system goes company-wide.

Feedback and Adjustment

Gathering feedback from the sales team on the ground allows leaders to adjust processes in real-time, ensuring that changes lead to genuine improvements in efficiency.

Example: After implementing new sales software, a sales leader holds feedback sessions to identify user issues and coordinates with the IT department to address them quickly.

Workshop Activities

Activity 1: Mapping the Sales Process

Participants map out their current sales process and identify areas where inefficiencies occur. This visual tool helps teams understand the flow of activities and pinpoint redundancies.

Activity 2: Automation Opportunity Workshop

Teams discuss and list daily tasks that could potentially be automated. Each team then proposes tools or solutions that could handle these tasks, evaluating their potential impact on productivity.

Activity 3: Lean Sales Simulation

In a simulation exercise, participants apply lean principles to redesign a segment of their sales process. This hands-on activity helps reinforce the principles of waste reduction and value enhancement.

Conclusion

Streamlining operations is crucial for maintaining a competitive edge in the fast-paced sales environment. This chapter provides sales leaders with a comprehensive framework for enhancing operational efficiency, supported by practical examples and interactive activities. By embracing these strategies, sales organizations can ensure their processes are not only efficient but also adaptable to the changing demands of the market.

CHAPTER 12

Technology in Sales: Leveraging Tools for Enhanced Performance

--- " ---

The right tools amplify your team's efforts, enabling smarter, faster, and more effective selling.

--- " ---

In today's competitive marketplace, leveraging technology is essential for enhancing sales performance. This chapter explores various sales technologies, from customer relationship management (CRM) systems to artificial intelligence (AI) tools, and how they can be effectively integrated into sales strategies to boost efficiency, improve accuracy, and drive sales growth.

The Role of Technology
in Modern Sales

Enhancing Data Management

Effective data management is critical for understanding customer behaviors and optimizing sales efforts. CRM systems play a pivotal role by aggregating and analyzing customer interactions, sales data, and market trends.

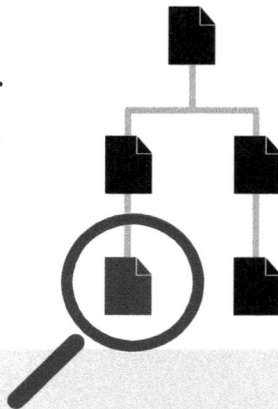

Example: A retail company uses a CRM to track customer purchase histories and preferences, which enables personalized marketing and has led to a 20% increase in customer retention rates.

Streamlining Communications

Technology facilitates quicker and more efficient communication with prospects and customers. Tools like automated email platforms and advanced messaging systems ensure consistent and timely interactions.

Example: A B2B company implements a chatbot on its website that handles initial customer inquiries and schedules appointments, freeing up sales staff to focus on higher-value activities.

Key Sales Technologies

Customer Relationship Management (CRM) Systems

CRMs are the backbone of modern sales technology, helping businesses manage leads, customer interactions, sales pipelines, and post-sale services in one centralized platform.

■ **Example:** A software solutions provider uses a CRM to segment customers based on usage patterns and tailors upsell strategies accordingly, significantly increasing upsell revenues.

Artificial Intelligence and Machine Learning

AI and machine learning can analyze vast amounts of data to identify patterns, predict customer behaviors, and automate repetitive tasks, thereby increasing accuracy and productivity.

■ **Example:** An e-commerce company employs machine learning algorithms to predict buying trends and adjust inventory levels in real-time, reducing stockouts and overstock situations.

Mobile Sales Applications

Mobile sales applications allow sales teams to access information and perform tasks on the go, increasing their agility and ability to respond to customer needs promptly.

■ **Example:** A pharmaceutical sales rep uses a mobile app to access drug information, update client records on the fly, and process orders directly from the field.

Implementing Sales Technology

Choosing the Right Tools

Selecting the right technology starts with a clear understanding of the business's specific needs and challenges. It involves evaluating different tools based on functionality, scalability, integration capabilities, and cost.

Example: A small startup chooses a cloud-based CRM that is affordable and can scale as the company grows, over more complex systems designed for larger enterprises.

Integration and Training

Successfully integrating new technology into existing sales processes is crucial. Comprehensive training programs ensure that sales teams can maximize the benefits of these tools.

Example: After implementing a new CRM system, a company conducts several training sessions and provides ongoing support to ensure all team members are proficient in using the new system.

Workshop Activities

Activity 1: Technology Audit

Participants assess their current technology stack to identify gaps and redundancies. This audit helps pinpoint areas where new technologies could improve efficiency and performance.

Activity 2: CRM Simulation

In this activity, teams use a demo CRM system to manage a fictional sales pipeline. This hands-on experience helps participants understand how CRMs can be used to streamline sales processes.

Activity 3: AI Impact Discussion

Teams discuss potential uses of AI in their sales processes, focusing on identifying tasks that AI could automate and how it could enhance decision-making through predictive analytics.

Conclusion

Incorporating technology into sales strategies is not just about keeping up with trends—it's about transforming how sales are managed and executed to drive significant improvements in performance. This chapter provides sales leaders with the knowledge and tools to assess, select, and implement technology solutions that will best fit their sales operations, supported by real-world examples and practical activities.

ADVANCED SALES LEADERSHIP

To truly elevate your leadership, you must go beyond the basics and embrace advanced principles that foster growth and innovation. This section explores the nuances of coaching and mentoring your team, using motivational techniques to inspire exceptional performance, and designing compensation plans that align incentives with goals. You'll also learn how to navigate change and build lasting relationships with customers. These chapters will help you refine your approach and develop a leadership style that drives sustained success.

CHAPTER 13

Coaching and Mentoring: Developing Your Team Through Continuous Learning

"

The best leaders don't just manage performance—
they shape careers and unlock potential.

"

In the fast-paced world of sales, continuous learning through effective coaching and mentoring is essential for maintaining competitiveness and fostering team growth. This chapter delves into the best practices for developing a continuous learning environment that nurtures skill enhancement and personal growth, ultimately leading to improved sales performance.

The Importance of
Coaching and Mentoring

Building a Culture of Growth

A culture that values continuous learning and development not only helps in retaining talent but also in attracting top performers who are eager to advance their careers. Coaching and mentoring play pivotal roles in this by providing regular opportunities for development and feedback.

Example: A technology sales company implements bi-weekly coaching sessions that focus on developing specific sales skills, such as negotiation or digital prospecting, resulting in a measurable uptick in sales performance metrics.

Adapting to Industry Changes

Sales environments are continually evolving due to new technologies, changing customer preferences, and competitive dynamics. Effective coaching helps sales teams adapt by ensuring they are always up-to-date with the latest industry trends and techniques.

Example: In response to a shift towards more value-based selling in the pharmaceutical industry, a sales leader introduces a mentoring program pairing new representatives with seasoned veterans to transfer knowledge about new selling techniques and regulatory considerations.

Strategies for Effective Coaching

Individualized Development Plans

Tailoring development plans to the individual needs of sales team members ensures that coaching and mentoring are relevant and effective. This involves assessing the strengths and weaknesses of each team member and creating a targeted plan to enhance their skills.

Example: A sales manager works with each team member to set personalized learning objectives based on their sales performance data and career aspirations, followed by regular check-ins to discuss progress and adjust the plan as needed.

Utilizing a Variety of Learning Methods

Incorporating different learning methods, such as one-on-one sessions, group training, peer learning, and digital courses, can cater to different learning styles and needs.

Example: A retail sales team uses a mix of role-playing workshops to practice customer interactions, e-learning modules for product knowledge, and group discussions to encourage sharing of sales tactics.

Fostering a Mentoring Environment

Peer Mentoring

Setting up peer mentoring within the sales team can enhance learning and build a supportive team environment. Experienced salespeople mentor newer employees, sharing knowledge and offering advice based on their own experiences.

■ **Example:** A real estate agency creates a buddy system where new agents are paired with experienced agents who provide guidance on everything from client management to closing techniques.

Formal and Informal Mentoring

While formal mentoring programs are structured and goal-oriented, informal mentoring can happen in day-to-day interactions and is equally valuable for spontaneous learning and support.

■ **Example:** An IT services company establishes a formal mentoring program with scheduled meetings and goals, alongside promoting an open-door policy for informal advice and support.

Workshop Activities

Activity 1: Creating Personalized Learning Plans

Participants work in small groups to help each other develop personalized learning plans. This includes identifying key areas for development, setting specific learning goals, and choosing appropriate learning methods and resources.

Activity 2: Role-Playing Coaching Scenarios

In this activity, participants take turns acting as a coach and a coachee, practicing their coaching techniques on various sales topics. Feedback from peers helps refine their approach.

Activity 3: Designing a Mentoring Program

Teams collaborate to design a formal mentoring program for their sales department. They define the program's structure, objectives, and matching criteria for mentors and mentees.

Conclusion

Coaching and mentoring are crucial for developing a knowledgeable and adaptable sales force. By investing in these areas, sales leaders can ensure their teams are well-equipped to meet current challenges and future opportunities. This chapter provides the strategies and tools necessary to implement effective coaching and mentoring programs, supported by practical examples and interactive workshop activities.

Motivational Techniques: Strategies to Inspire and Drive Your Team to Exceed Targets

"

Motivation isn't about pushing harder—it's about inspiring your team to want to excel.

"

Motivation is a key driver of sales performance, influencing how effectively a team meets and exceeds their targets. This chapter explores various motivational techniques that sales leaders can use to inspire their teams, foster a high-energy sales environment, and achieve exceptional results.

Understanding Motivation in Sales

The Role of Motivation

Motivation in sales is multifaceted, encompassing intrinsic drivers like personal achievement and extrinsic factors such as rewards and recognition. Understanding what motivates each team member is crucial for tailoring strategies that resonate on an individual level.

Example: A sales leader notices that while some team members are motivated by cash bonuses, others value public recognition or opportunities for professional development.

Linking Motivation to Performance

Effective motivation directly impacts sales performance by increasing engagement and commitment to organizational goals. It's about aligning team members' personal goals with the goals of the organization.

Example: During annual reviews, a sales manager aligns individual sales targets with career advancement paths, showing team members how meeting sales goals can lead to personal career growth.

Motivational Strategies

Setting Clear Goals and Expectations

Clear, achievable goals give team members direction and a sense of purpose. These should be specific, measurable, attainable, relevant, and time-bound (SMART).

- **Example:** A sales leader sets quarterly sales goals for each team member, accompanied by specific strategies on how to achieve them, and regularly monitors progress.

Recognition and Rewards

Implementing a recognition and rewards system that acknowledges both team and individual achievements can significantly boost morale and motivation.

- **Example:** An IT company uses a point system where sales reps earn points for activities that align with company values and goals. These points can be exchanged for various rewards, from gift cards to extra vacation days.

Creating Competitive but Collaborative Environments

While competition can be a strong motivator, balancing it with collaboration ensures that the sales environment remains positive and team-oriented.

- **Example:** A monthly sales contest rewards the highest-performing team rather than individual salespeople, encouraging teamwork and peer support.

Enhancing Intrinsic Motivation

Career Development Opportunities

Providing opportunities for professional development can motivate team members by demonstrating the company's investment in their personal and professional growth.

> **Example:** A pharmaceutical sales company offers access to advanced sales training courses and certifications for team members who meet specific performance thresholds.

Empowering Team Members

Empowerment is a powerful motivator. Sales leaders who delegate authority and trust their team members to make decisions tend to see higher engagement and initiative.

> **Example:** A sales leader allows team members to negotiate deals up to a certain dollar amount without prior approval, giving them a sense of autonomy and responsibility.

Workshop Activities

Activity 1: Goal-Setting Workshop

Participants engage in a workshop to set their personal and team goals for the quarter. They learn how to make these goals SMART and align them with their personal career aspirations.

Activity 2: Rewards Program Design

Teams work together to create or redesign a rewards and recognition program for their sales department. They consider what types of behaviors they want to encourage, as well as the preferences and motivations of their team members.

Activity 3: Role-Play on Empowerment Scenarios

Participants role-play various scenarios where they must make decisions independently. This helps them build confidence in their decision-making skills and understand the impact of empowerment on motivation.

Conclusion

Motivating a sales team involves a mix of understanding individual motivators, setting appropriate and clear goals, recognizing achievements, and fostering a supportive and empowering work environment. This chapter provides sales leaders with a comprehensive understanding of different motivational strategies and practical activities to help implement these strategies effectively, ensuring their teams remain driven and focused on exceeding targets.

CHAPTER 15

Designing Effective Sales Compensation Plans: Aligning Incentives with Goals

"

Compensation plans must align incentives with goals, motivating your team to achieve the right outcomes.

"

Effective sales compensation plans are critical in motivating sales teams and aligning their efforts with organizational goals. This chapter explores various compensation models, each illustrated with examples using real numbers to help you understand and implement plans that enhance performance and reward achievements.

Understanding Sales Compensation Structures

The Role of Compensation in Sales

Compensation influences sales behaviors, directs efforts towards strategic priorities, shapes team culture, and aligns individual achievements with company goals.

Key Sales Compensation Models and Their Implications

1. Salary Only

- **Description:** Sales representatives receive a fixed salary with no commission or bonuses.
- **Example:** A sales rep earns a steady salary of $50,000 annually, regardless of sales volume.
- **Pros:** Provides income stability, reduces stress, and encourages customer service focus.
- **Cons:** May not motivate reps to exceed sales targets, potentially leading to lower sales activity.

2. Straight Commission

- **Description:** Compensation is entirely based on sales performance, with no base salary.
- **Example:** A real estate agent earns a 3% commission on each property sold. If they sell a house priced at $300,000, they earn $9,000 from that sale.
- **Pros:** Maximizes motivation for high performers.
- **Cons:** Can lead to income instability and high stress.

3. Salary Plus Bonuses

- **Description:** A base salary supplemented by bonuses tied to performance milestones.
- **Example:** A sales rep earns a base salary of $40,000 plus a $5,000 bonus for every $100,000 in sales beyond the first $300,000 annually.
- **Pros:** Ensures financial stability while motivating performance.
- **Cons:** Bonuses must be well-structured to effectively motivate desired behaviors.

4. Benchmark-based Commission

- **Description:** Commission is paid only after reaching a predefined sales threshold or benchmark.
- **Example:** A sales rep earns a 10% commission on all sales after exceeding a quarterly benchmark of $50,000. Sales up to that point do not earn commission.
- **Pros:** Encourages minimum standard achievement.
- **Cons:** High benchmarks may demotivate those who find them unattainable.

5. Draw Against Commission

- **Description:** A regular advance or "draw" is provided, which is later offset against earned commissions.
- **Example:** A new sales rep receives a monthly draw of $2,000. If they earn $3,000 in commissions in a month, the first $2,000 covers the draw, and they receive an additional $1,000.
- **Pros:** Provides income stability for new reps.
- **Cons:** Reps must manage their finances to avoid repayment issues if commissions don't cover the draw.

6. Profit Sharing

- **Description:** A portion of company profits is distributed to employees, typically based on their performance or tenure.
- **Example:** A company offers 2% of annual profits as a bonus to sales teams. If the company's profit is $1 million, the sales team shares $20,000.
- **Pros:** Aligns the interests of the employees with the company's profitability.
- **Cons:** The link between individual performance and rewards can be indirect.

7. Set Rate Commission

- **Description:** A fixed rate of commission on all sales, regardless of volume or profit margins.
- **Example:** A car salesman earns a flat 5% commission on each car sold. If they sell a car for $20,000, they earn $1,000.
- **Pros:** Simple to understand and administer.
- **Cons:** Does not incentivize selling higher-margin products.

8. Equity

- **Description:** Offering stock options or shares in the company, typically to senior sales executives or high performers.
- **Example:** A senior sales executive is granted 1,000 shares of company stock as part of their compensation, vesting over four years.
- **Pros:** Provides long-term motivation and aligns sales executives' interests with those of shareholders.
- **Cons:** Benefits may be realized in the long term and are dependent on company success.

9. Territory Volume Incentive

- **Description:** Commission based on total sales within a specific geographic territory, regardless of individual performance.
- **Example:** Sales teams in the Northeast region earn a 2% commission on total regional sales, which total $500,000, thus earning $10,000 to be divided among the team.
- **Pros:** Promotes teamwork and cooperative efforts.
- **Cons:** Can overlook individual contributions.

10. Merit Pay

- **Description:** Additional pay based on performance reviews, considering factors beyond sales numbers, like customer service and teamwork.
- **Example:** A sales rep earns a base salary and can receive up to a 5% increase ($2,500 on a $50,000 salary) based on annual performance evaluations.
- **Pros:** Encourages a broad range of performance metrics.
- **Cons:** Subjectivity in performance evaluations can lead to perceptions of unfairness.

Implementing and Managing Compensation Plans

Communication and Transparency

Clear communication about how compensation plans work is essential. Sales teams must understand how their efforts translate into earnings.

Monitoring and Flexibility

Regular reviews and adjustments based on effectiveness and market conditions are crucial to maintain motivation and align with business goals.

Workshop Activities

Activity 1: Compensation Design Workshop

Participants use real sales data to design compensation plans for a hypothetical company, selecting models that align with specific business scenarios and goals.

Activity 2: Compensation Plan Analysis

Teams analyze existing compensation plans using real-world numbers, identifying impacts on sales performance and employee satisfaction.

Activity 3: Role-Playing Sales Scenarios

Teams role-play as salespeople under different compensation models to explore how these models influence their strategies and customer interactions, using concrete numbers to simulate earnings.

Conclusion

Selecting the right sales compensation model is essential for motivating sales teams and achieving business objectives. This chapter provides a comprehensive guide to understanding, selecting, and implementing effective compensation strategies tailored to various sales environments, complete with real-world examples and numerical illustrations to clarify how different plans work in practice.

Change Management: Leading Your Team Through Shifts in Strategy and Market Conditions

"

Leading through change requires clarity, empathy, and a steadfast commitment to your team's success.

"

Change management is critical in sales, where market conditions and strategic directions can shift rapidly. Effective leadership through these changes ensures that teams remain resilient, adaptive, and focused. This chapter explores strategies for leading sales teams through significant changes, including shifts in market conditions, strategic pivots, and organizational restructuring.

Understanding the Impact of Change

The Nature of Change in Sales

In the dynamic world of sales, change is inevitable. Whether due to technological advancements, competitive pressures, or evolving customer preferences, sales teams must continuously adapt to maintain their edge.

> **Example:** A consumer electronics company must rapidly shift its sales strategy in response to unexpected technological innovations by a competitor.

Psychological Impact on Teams

Change can be unsettling, leading to resistance among team members. Understanding and addressing the psychological impact of change is crucial for maintaining morale and productivity.

> **Example:** A sales team shows signs of stress and decreased performance following the announcement of a merger that could alter their sales territories and quotas.

Strategies for Effective Change Management

Communicating Change

Clear, transparent communication is the foundation of effective change management. Leaders must explain the reasons for changes, how they will impact the team, and the expected benefits.

Example: When introducing a new sales CRM system, the sales leader holds a meeting to discuss how this change will streamline processes and ultimately ease the workload on sales reps.

Involving the Team in the Change Process

Involving team members in planning and implementing change increases buy-in and reduces resistance. It gives the team a sense of control and ownership over the change.

Example: Before restructuring the sales department, the leader forms a committee of sales reps to provide input on how the restructuring can best support their work.

Providing Training and Support

Offering adequate training and support during transitions is essential. This ensures that all team members feel equipped to handle new systems, processes, or strategies.

Example: A company rolling out a new product line provides extensive product training and sales techniques workshops to ensure the sales team is confident and knowledgeable.

Monitoring and Adjusting

Continuous monitoring of how changes are affecting the team and the sales outcomes is vital. Being prepared to make adjustments based on feedback and performance metrics ensures the change process aligns with desired outcomes.

> **Example:** After implementing a new sales strategy, sales performance metrics are closely monitored, and strategy tweaks are made to address areas where targets are not being met.

Workshop
Activities

Activity 1: Role-Playing Change Scenarios

Participants engage in role-playing exercises to act out different change scenarios, such as announcing a new sales strategy or responding to a hypothetical market downturn. This helps develop their skills in handling questions and resistance from the team.

Activity 2: Developing a Change Communication Plan

Teams work together to create a communication plan for a significant organizational change, such as a merger or acquisition. They must consider the timing of communications, the platforms to be used, and the key messages to be conveyed.

Activity 3: Change Leadership Simulation

In this simulation, participants take on leadership roles during a major strategic shift. They must manage their virtual teams through the change, making decisions on communication, training, and adjustment based on simulated team feedback and performance data.

Conclusion

Leading a sales team through change requires more than just managerial skills; it demands a deep understanding of the human aspects of change, strategic communication, and the ability to adapt and respond to feedback. This chapter equips sales leaders with the tools and insights needed to manage change effectively, ensuring their teams can navigate transitions smoothly and continue to perform at high levels.

CHAPTER 17

Customer Relationship Leadership: Cultivating Key Relationships for Long-Term Success

> ❝
>
> *Strong customer relationships aren't just built—they're cultivated through trust, value, and consistency.*
>
> ❞

In the competitive realm of sales, customer relationships are a cornerstone of long-term success. Effective customer relationship leadership not only drives immediate sales but also builds a foundation for sustained growth and customer loyalty. This chapter delves into strategies for leading a sales team in a manner that prioritizes and enhances customer relationships, with a focus on leveraging these relationships to achieve strategic business objectives.

The Importance of
Customer Relationships

Defining Customer Relationship Leadership

Customer relationship leadership involves guiding sales teams to build and maintain strong, trust-based relationships with clients. It extends beyond typical sales interactions to involve strategic account management and high-level engagement.

Example: A sales leader at a software company develops a program that assigns account managers to high-value clients, focusing on understanding and meeting their unique business needs.

Impact on Business Outcomes

Strong customer relationships can lead to repeat business, referrals, and increased customer lifetime value. They serve as a competitive differentiator in crowded markets.

Example: By consistently engaging with key clients and offering tailored solutions, a manufacturing company secures a renewal rate of over 90% on contracts.

Strategies for Enhancing
Customer Relationships

Personalized Engagement

Understanding and addressing the specific needs and preferences of each customer can significantly enhance relationship quality. Personalized engagement involves customized communications, tailored solutions, and proactive service.

■ **Example:** A B2B service provider uses customer data to anticipate needs and proactively offers solutions before the customer initiates contact.

Empowering Teams to Build Relationships

Sales leaders must empower their teams by providing the tools, resources, and autonomy needed to nurture relationships. This includes training on relationship-building skills and the use of CRM systems to manage and analyze customer interactions effectively.

■ **Example:** A sales leader implements a flexible policy that allows sales reps to offer custom discounts or service enhancements to long-term clients, strengthening loyalty.

Consistency and Reliability

Being consistent and reliable in all interactions with customers builds trust over time. This means ensuring that the sales team follows through on promises and maintains a consistent level of service.

■ **Example:** A retail company trains its sales staff to ensure that customer service levels are uniform across all stores and touchpoints, reinforcing brand reliability.

Leveraging Technology

Using technology to enhance customer relationships is crucial. CRM systems, data analytics, and mobile sales tools can provide deeper insights into customer preferences and behaviors, facilitating more effective engagement.

Example: A technology firm uses advanced analytics to segment customers based on purchasing behavior, allowing sales reps to personalize interactions and offers.

Workshop
Activities

Activity 1: Building Personalized Engagement Plans

Participants work in groups to create detailed engagement plans for different types of customers, focusing on personalization and proactive service strategies.

Activity 2: Role-Playing Customer Interactions

Teams role-play various scenarios to practice handling customer interactions, including difficult conversations, negotiating deals, and delivering customized solutions.

Activity 3: CRM Training Simulation

In a hands-on session, participants learn to use a CRM platform to record customer interactions, analyze customer data, and use insights to drive decisions about relationship management.

Conclusion

Effective customer relationship leadership is vital for cultivating long-term, profitable customer relationships. By focusing on personalized engagement, empowering teams, ensuring consistency, and effectively using technology, sales leaders can guide their teams to success in a competitive market. This chapter provides a comprehensive guide to understanding and implementing strategies that deepen customer connections and drive sustained business growth.

MANAGING TALENT AND CHALLENGES IN SALES TEAMS

Leading a sales team means managing both opportunities and obstacles. In this section, we'll tackle some of the toughest challenges sales leaders face, from identifying and addressing problematic behavior to discovering hidden talent and developing future leaders. You'll learn how to balance your focus between nurturing rising stars and managing challenging personalities. These chapters offer actionable strategies for building a team that thrives in any situation, ensuring both individual and collective success.

Identifying Problematic Behavior: Recognizing Signs of Underperformance and Negativity That Can Affect Team Dynamics

---

"

Recognizing early signs of negativity and underperformance is key to protecting team dynamics and results.

"

In any sales team, identifying and addressing problematic behaviors early is crucial to maintaining a positive work environment and achieving collective goals. This chapter explores the common signs of underperformance and negativity within sales teams, offering strategies for recognizing these behaviors and effectively addressing them to prevent disruption of team dynamics.

Understanding
Problematic Behaviors

Defining Problematic Behavior

Problematic behavior in a sales context can range from underperformance, such as consistently failing to meet sales targets, to negative attitudes that can poison team morale, such as gossiping, non-cooperation, or overt conflict.

Example: A sales rep consistently misses monthly sales goals and displays a cynical attitude during team meetings, undermining team morale.

Impact on Team Dynamics

Such behaviors can lead to decreased overall team performance, affect customer relationships, and create a toxic work environment, ultimately threatening team cohesion and company culture.

Example: Persistent negativity from one team member leads to increased stress levels among other team members, resulting in higher absenteeism and decreased productivity.

Signs of Problematic Behavior

1. Decline in Performance

A sudden or gradual decline in performance, such as not reaching sales quotas or decreased customer engagement, can be a sign of underlying issues.

> **Example:** A previously high-performing salesperson shows a noticeable decline in sales over two consecutive quarters without any apparent external factors.

2. Withdrawal from Team Activities

Withdrawing from team meetings, training sessions, or other collaborative activities can indicate disengagement or dissatisfaction.

> **Example:** A team member who used to actively participate in weekly brainstorming sessions starts to withdraw and becomes noticeably disinterested.

3. Changes in Attitude

Changes in attitude, including increased cynicism, negative comments about the company or clients, or a general lack of enthusiasm, can be early warning signs of deeper issues.

> **Example:** A sales rep begins to express skepticism about the effectiveness of new sales strategies and openly criticizes management decisions.

4. Interpersonal Conflicts

Frequent conflicts with colleagues or supervisors, reluctance to collaborate, or complaints from other team members can indicate problematic behavior.

> **Example:** Multiple team members report feeling uncomfortable working with a particular colleague due to their confrontational style.

Addressing Problematic Behaviors

Early Intervention

Addressing issues early can prevent them from escalating and affecting the wider team. Regular one-on-one meetings can help managers catch and address these behaviors promptly.

- **Example:** A sales manager schedules monthly one-on-one check-ins with each team member to discuss their concerns and performance issues.

Constructive Feedback

Providing constructive feedback in a supportive manner can help individuals recognize and correct their behavior before it becomes a more significant issue.

- **Example:** During a performance review, a manager discusses specific instances of the problematic behavior and collaborates with the employee to develop an improvement plan.

Training and Support

Offering additional training and support can help struggling team members improve their performance and attitude, demonstrating the organization's commitment to their success.

- **Example:** A salesperson showing signs of burnout is offered sessions with a career coach and time management training.

Workshop

Activities

Activity 1: Role-Playing Intervention Strategies

Participants role-play various scenarios of problematic behaviors, practicing how to intervene effectively and provide constructive feedback.

Activity 2: Creating an Action Plan for Problematic Behaviors

Teams work together to create action plans for hypothetical scenarios involving underperformance and negativity, focusing on early intervention and support.

Activity 3: Developing Emotional Intelligence Skills

A workshop focused on developing emotional intelligence to better understand and respond to signs of disengagement and negativity among team members.

Conclusion

Identifying and addressing problematic behavior in sales teams is essential for maintaining a positive and productive work environment. This chapter provides a detailed guide on recognizing the signs of such behaviors and effectively managing them through proactive leadership and supportive strategies. These approaches help sustain team dynamics and drive success in a competitive sales environment.

CHAPTER 19

Effective Remediation Strategies: Approaches to Coach and Improve Problematic Sellers or Decide When to Part Ways

"

The choice to coach or cut a problematic seller can define the trajectory of your team's success.

"

Managing underperforming sales representatives is a critical aspect of sales leadership. Effective remediation strategies not only aim to improve performance but also ensure that the team's overall productivity and morale are maintained. This chapter outlines methods for coaching underperforming sellers, identifies signs when it may be necessary to part ways, and provides guidelines for doing so compassionately and legally.

Understanding the Dynamics
of Underperformance

Identifying the Root Causes

Before addressing underperformance, it's essential to understand its causes, which can range from personal issues and skill gaps to misalignment with company culture or unclear job expectations.

Example: A sales rep's performance might decline after new software is introduced, indicating a potential skill gap rather than a lack of effort.

Impact on the Team

Underperformance can affect more than just individual results; it can impact team morale and productivity, making it crucial for leaders to address these issues promptly and effectively.

Example: Continuous underperformance from one team member can lead to increased workload and stress on other team members, potentially causing overall team burnout.

Strategies for Coaching
Underperforming Sellers

1. Tailored Coaching Plans

Develop individualized coaching plans based on the specific needs and weaknesses of the sales representative. This approach should include achievable milestones and regular feedback sessions.

■ **Example:** For a rep struggling with closing deals, a manager might set up bi-weekly role-play sessions to practice closing techniques and handle objections.

2. Training and Development

Invest in targeted training programs to help underperforming reps improve their skills. This could include formal training sessions, workshops, or access to new learning resources.

■ **Example:** A sales rep having difficulty with product knowledge might benefit from additional product training sessions or partnering with a product specialist.

3. Performance Improvement Plans (PIPs)

Implement Performance Improvement Plans that clearly outline expected improvements, provide a timeline for achieving these improvements, and detail the support available to the employee.

■ **Example:** A PIP might stipulate that a sales rep needs to increase their sales figures by 20% over three months, with specific steps and support outlined to achieve this goal.

Deciding When to Part Ways

Recognizing When It's Time

Despite best efforts, there may come a time when parting ways is the best option for both the company and the employee. Signs include a consistent inability to meet PIP objectives, detrimental effects on team morale, or a clear misfit with company culture.

■ **Example:** After several months on a PIP and multiple coaching attempts, if the sales rep's performance does not improve to meet minimum standards, it may be time to discuss separation.

Conducting Compassionate Offboarding

When separation becomes necessary, it's important to handle the process with respect and compassion, providing support such as career counseling or assistance in finding new job opportunities.

■ **Example:** Offer a severance package and professional outplacement services to help the departing sales rep transition to a new career opportunity.

Workshop
Activities

Activity 1: Developing Coaching Plans

Participants design coaching plans for different types of underperforming sales scenarios. This activity helps managers tailor interventions based on specific performance issues.

Activity 2: Role-Playing Performance Conversations

Teams role-play conversations between managers

and underperforming reps, practicing how to deliver feedback constructively and set up PIPs effectively.

Activity 3: Navigating Difficult Decisions

A workshop to explore scenarios where parting ways is necessary, focusing on how to handle these conversations ethically and compassionately.

Conclusion

Effectively managing underperforming sales representatives requires a balanced approach of targeted coaching, timely interventions, and, when necessary, making the difficult decision to part ways. By employing the strategies outlined in this chapter, sales leaders can ensure they are providing every opportunity for team members to succeed while also maintaining the health and productivity of the sales team.

CHAPTER 20

Legal and Ethical Considerations: Navigating the Legalities of Dismissal and the Ethics of Personnel Management

"

Navigating personnel decisions ethically and legally protects your team, your organization, and your integrity.

"

Handling the legal and ethical aspects of personnel management, especially dismissal, is crucial for maintaining a fair, respectful, and legally compliant workplace. This chapter provides an in-depth analysis of the legal frameworks governing dismissal and the ethical considerations that should guide personnel decisions. It includes practical examples and workshop activities to help sales leaders navigate these complex areas effectively.

Understanding Legal Grounds for Dismissal

Employment Laws and Regulations

Familiarity with employment laws such as the Fair Labor Standards Act (FLSA), Americans with Disabilities Act (ADA), and others is essential for ensuring that dismissals are legally justified and executed properly.

■ **Example:** A sales manager must understand the legal protections around disability to ensure that a dismissal related to performance is not inadvertently discriminating against an employee's protected disability status.

At-Will vs. Contractual Employment

Differentiating between at-will and contractual employment is crucial, as the terms of dismissal can vary significantly. At-will employment allows employers and employees to end employment without cause, but there are exceptions based on state laws and public policy.

■ **Example:** In an at-will state, a sales employee can generally be dismissed without cause, but not for reasons that violate anti-discrimination laws.

Ethical Considerations in Dismissal

Fairness and Transparency

Ethical dismissals are grounded in fairness, transparency, and respect. Ensuring that all employees are treated equally and that the reasons for dismissal are clear and justifiable is fundamental.

■ **Example:** Before deciding to dismiss a sales rep for underperformance, the manager ensures that the employee had received clear performance targets, adequate feedback, and opportunities to improve.

Communication and Privacy

Maintaining privacy and dignity during the dismissal process is not only a legal requirement but also an ethical obligation. How a dismissal is communicated can significantly affect the remaining team's morale and the company's reputation.

■ **Example:** A sales leader conducts dismissal meetings in a private setting, providing the employee with a clear explanation and avoiding unnecessary embarrassment or disclosure to other employees.

Navigating Dismissal Procedures

Documenting Performance Issues

Thorough documentation of performance issues and disciplinary actions is essential for legal and ethical dismissals. This documentation should be factual, consistent, and free of any subjective or discriminatory language.

■ **Example:** The sales manager keeps detailed records of performance reviews, meetings, and correspondences discussing performance issues with the employee.

Implementing Fair Procedures

Adhering to established procedures for warnings, performance improvement plans (PIPs), and reviews ensures that dismissals are not arbitrary but are the result of a fair and systematic process.

Example: A sales rep who fails to meet their targets is given a 60-day PIP with specific, measurable objectives and regular check-ins before any final dismissal decision is made.

Workshop Activities

Activity 1: Role-Playing Dismissal Scenarios

Participants role-play various dismissal scenarios to practice delivering difficult news ethically and legally. Scenarios include handling dismissals for different causes such as economic layoffs, performance issues, and misconduct.

Activity 2: Legal Quiz on Employment Laws

A quiz or interactive session to test knowledge of relevant employment laws and best practices in handling dismissals, helping participants identify areas where they need more understanding or training.

Activity 3: Developing Ethical Guidelines for Dismissal

Teams work together to develop or refine their organization's ethical guidelines for dismissals, focusing on transparency, fairness, and respect for privacy.

Conclusion

Navigating the legalities of dismissal and the ethics of personnel management requires careful attention to legal standards and a strong commitment to ethical principles. By understanding and implementing the strategies discussed in this chapter, sales leaders can ensure that dismissals are conducted legally and ethically, thereby protecting the organization and its employees while maintaining a positive and productive work environment.

CHAPTER 21

Discovering Hidden Talent: Techniques for Spotting Potential in Overlooked Team Members

"

Potential often hides in plain sight—your job is to find it and give it the opportunity to shine.

"

In every sales team, some members naturally stand out while others may not immediately showcase their potential. Discovering and nurturing hidden talent within the team is crucial for enhancing productivity and fostering a competitive and inclusive workplace. This chapter explores techniques for identifying and developing the potential of overlooked team members, ensuring that no reservoir of talent goes untapped.

Understanding Hidden Talent

Defining Hidden Talent

Hidden talent refers to those team members who possess significant skills or potential that have not been fully utilized or recognized. These individuals often require targeted support to unlock their capabilities and contribute effectively to team goals.

Example: A sales team member who excels in technical knowledge but has yet to translate this skill into sales leadership or strategy might be considered a hidden talent.

Benefits of Uncovering Hidden Talent

Leveraging the full range of talents within a team can lead to increased innovation, better team dynamics, and enhanced overall performance. It also boosts morale and retention by showing team members that the organization values growth and development for everyone.

Example: By identifying and nurturing a quiet team member's analytic skills, a sales manager can fill a crucial gap in data-driven sales strategies, benefiting the entire team.

Techniques for Identifying Hidden Talent

1. Skills Assessments

Regular skills assessments can help leaders identify abilities that are not being used to their fullest potential. These assessments should cover a variety of areas, including both hard and soft skills.

- **Example:** Implementing annual skills assessments that test not only sales-specific skills but also leadership, communication, and analytical abilities.

2. Providing Diverse Opportunities

Offering a variety of projects and roles can expose hidden strengths among team members. Encouraging participation in cross-departmental projects can also help in discovering and utilizing unseen talents.

- **Example:** Rotating team members through different sales roles, such as client management, negotiation, and after-sales service, to reveal previously unnoticed competencies.

3. Encouraging Self-Advocacy

Create an environment where team members feel comfortable advocating for themselves and discussing their interests and hidden skills with management.

- **Example:** Hosting regular career development meetings where team members can discuss their career aspirations and potential interests beyond their current roles.

Developing Hidden Talent

Tailored Development Programs

Once hidden talents are identified, personalized development programs can help individuals enhance their skills and increase their contribution to the team.

Example: Designing a mentorship program for a team member who has shown potential in leadership, pairing them with experienced leaders within the organization.

Recognition and Encouragement

Recognizing and rewarding the development and use of new skills can motivate other team members to share and develop their hidden talents.

Example: Publicly acknowledging a team member's successful management of a challenging project during a team meeting, and rewarding them with a leadership role in an upcoming high-profile project.

Workshop
Activities

Activity 1: Talent Discovery Workshop

Participants engage in a workshop where they complete skills assessments and receive feedback that helps them understand their hidden talents and how these can be developed.

Activity 2: Role-Playing for Self-Advocacy

Teams role-play scenarios that involve advocating for new roles or projects based on their interests and hidden skills, practicing how to effectively communicate their capabilities to leadership.

Activity 3: Designing Personal Development Plans

In groups, participants use the results of their skills assessments to design personalized development plans, with guidance from facilitators on setting realistic and strategic career goals.

Conclusion

Uncovering and nurturing hidden talent within sales teams not only optimizes resources but also contributes to a more dynamic and innovative work environment. This chapter provides detailed strategies and practical examples for identifying, developing, and leveraging the diverse talents of all team members, ensuring that every individual has the opportunity to shine and contribute to the team's success.

CHAPTER 22

Developing Emerging Leaders: Investing in Promising Individuals with Tailored Growth Plans and Leadership Training

"

Investing in tomorrow's leaders ensures your team's success long after you've moved on.

"

Fostering emerging leaders within a sales team is crucial for sustaining long-term organizational success and innovation. This chapter outlines strategies for identifying and nurturing potential leaders by providing them with the skills and opportunities needed to grow into influential positions. By investing in tailored growth plans and leadership training, companies can ensure a continuous pipeline of capable leaders.

Identifying Potential Leaders

Traits of Emerging Leaders

Emerging leaders often exhibit traits such as proactivity, strong communication skills, problem-solving abilities, and a natural influence over peers. Identifying these traits early helps in targeting the right individuals for leadership development.

Example: A sales representative who regularly takes initiative to mentor new team members and has successfully led several team projects might be a candidate for leadership development.

Using Performance Metrics

Performance metrics can provide objective criteria to help identify potential leaders. High sales numbers are a starting point, but other metrics like customer satisfaction scores and the ability to meet strategic goals should also be considered.

Example: A sales manager uses a combination of sales performance data and 360-degree feedback to identify team members who consistently exceed targets and demonstrate leadership qualities in team settings.

Tailoring Growth Plans

Personalized Development Programs

Each potential leader has unique strengths and areas for improvement. Personalized development programs can address these individual needs, ensuring more effective growth.

> **Example:** For a salesperson excelling in operational efficiency but lacking experience in strategic decision-making, the development program might focus on strategic leadership training.

Mentorship and Coaching

Pairing emerging leaders with experienced mentors can accelerate their development. Mentors provide guidance, feedback, and support, helping mentees navigate the complexities of leadership roles.

> **Example:** An experienced sales executive mentors a high-potential sales agent, offering regular one-on-one coaching sessions and shadowing opportunities to provide insights into the nuances of higher-level management.

Leadership Training Programs

Formal Training Sessions

Structured training sessions that cover essential leadership skills such as conflict resolution, team management, and effective communication are crucial for developing well-rounded leaders.

> **Example:** A series of workshops focusing on leadership fundamentals, advanced negotiation techniques, and change management is offered to identified emerging leaders within the sales department.

Experiential Learning

Real-world leadership experiences can be invaluable. Providing emerging leaders with the opportunity to lead projects or temporary teams helps them apply their training in practical settings.

Example: An emerging leader is given the responsibility to lead a new market entry project, overseeing a small team and managing the budget and strategy execution.

Workshop
Activities

Activity 1: Leadership Trait Assessment

Participants complete assessments that help them identify their own leadership traits and areas for improvement. This activity includes feedback from peers and supervisors to ensure a comprehensive evaluation.

Activity 2: Role-Playing Leadership Challenges

Participants engage in role-playing exercises designed to simulate typical leadership challenges, such as handling an underperforming team member or managing a conflict within the team.

Activity 3: Developing Personal Leadership Plans

In this workshop, participants use insights from their assessments and role-playing exercises to create personalized leadership development plans. These plans outline specific goals, the training needed, and timelines for achieving leadership milestones.

Conclusion

Developing emerging leaders is essential for ensuring the continuity and growth of leadership within any sales organization. By identifying potential leaders early and investing in tailored growth plans and comprehensive leadership training, organizations can build a robust leadership pipeline that is ready to take on future challenges. This chapter provides a structured approach to nurturing the leadership potential of promising team members, enhancing the overall strategic capacity of the sales team.

CHAPTER 23

Balancing Focus: Allocating Your Energy Wisely Between Nurturing Rising Stars and Managing Challenging Personalities

"

Your energy is limited; invest it wisely in the people and strategies that yield the greatest return.

"

Effective leadership in a sales environment involves not only nurturing high performers but also managing those with challenging personalities or who are underperforming. Striking the right balance in allocating energy and resources between these groups is crucial for maintaining team harmony and optimizing overall performance. This chapter explores strategies for effectively balancing focus to ensure all team members are adequately supported and motivated.

Understanding the Dynamics of Team Management

Recognizing Diverse Needs

Every sales team is a blend of individuals with varying abilities, motivations, and challenges. Understanding and acknowledging these differences is the first step in effectively managing them.

Example: A team leader notices that while some team members excel in fast-paced sales environments, others perform best with long-term nurturing clients, indicating a need for tailored management strategies.

The Impact of Balanced Leadership

Balanced leadership promotes a more inclusive and equitable environment, which can lead to higher job satisfaction and lower turnover rates. It helps ensure that high performers continue to thrive without leaving behind those who may need more guidance.

Example: A sales manager creates a rotational mentoring program allowing high performers to mentor those struggling, which helps distribute leadership responsibilities and fosters a supportive team culture.

Strategies for Balancing Focus

1. Tailored Incentives

Develop incentive programs that reward various types of contributions, not just top sales numbers. This approach recognizes different strengths and motivations within the team.

- **Example:** Besides commission for sales, introduce rewards for best customer feedback, most improved, and best team player.

2. Segmented Team Management

Consider segmenting the team based on needs and providing different types of support to each segment. This allows leaders to focus their energy more effectively and meet individual team members where they are.

- **Example:** Establish separate weekly meetings for rising stars focused on advanced sales strategies, while another meeting might address foundational selling skills for those struggling.

3. Effective Delegation

Delegating appropriate responsibilities to trusted team members can free up management to focus more on individuals who require intensive coaching or mentorship.

- **Example:** A seasoned team member is tasked with leading routine team meetings, allowing the manager to spend more time on one-on-one coaching sessions.

4. Utilizing Peer Support

Encourage peer mentoring and support networks within the team. This not only helps distribute the leadership burden but also builds a more cohesive and mutually supportive team.

Example: Pair each challenging personality or underperformer with a rising star, promoting mutual learning and understanding.

Managing Challenging
Personalities

Addressing Issues Head-On

Early and direct intervention can prevent minor issues from becoming major disruptions. Regular feedback and open communication are key.

■ **Example:** A manager promptly addresses a team member who frequently interrupts colleagues, discussing the impact of such behavior on team dynamics and offering constructive ways to improve.

Personalized Development Plans

Create personalized plans that address specific behaviors and set clear, achievable goals for improvement.

■ **Example:** For a team member struggling with time management, a detailed plan including time management training and regular check-ins is developed.

Workshop
Activities

Activity 1: Role-Playing Management Scenarios

Participants role-play various scenarios, such as delivering feedback to a challenging personality or motivating an underperformer, to practice balancing leadership focus.

Activity 2: Designing Tailored Incentive Programs

Teams work together to create incentive programs that reward a variety of achievements, fostering a more balanced focus on different types of team contributions.

Activity 3: Developing Segmentation Strategies

In this activity, participants develop strategies for segmenting their team according to different needs and plan how to manage each segment effectively.

Conclusion

Balancing the focus between nurturing rising stars and managing challenging personalities requires thoughtful strategies and a deep understanding of individual team dynamics. By implementing tailored management approaches, leaders can ensure that all team members feel valued and supported, contributing to a more productive and harmonious workplace. This chapter provides essential insights and practical tools to help sales leaders achieve this balance effectively.

SECTION 6

SUSTAINING SUCCESS

The mark of a great sales leader isn't just achieving results—it's sustaining them. In this final section, we'll focus on how to measure performance, foster a culture of continuous improvement, and build a legacy that lasts. You'll also explore how to prepare for the future of sales leadership by staying ahead of emerging trends and opportunities. These chapters will challenge you to think beyond the present and create systems, relationships, and cultures that endure long after your tenure as a leader.

CHAPTER 24

Measuring Performance: Metrics That Matter for Sales Leadership

> ❝
> *What gets measured gets improved—track the metrics that matter and act on the insights they provide.*
> ❞

Effective sales leadership relies on data-driven decision-making, and performance metrics are at the heart of this process. Metrics provide insights into individual and team performance, operational efficiency, and the overall success of sales strategies. This chapter explores key sales metrics, their relevance, and how to leverage them to drive success. Practical examples and workshop activities are included to help leaders effectively measure and interpret performance.

The Importance of Performance Metrics

Data-Driven Decision-Making

Metrics offer objective insights that guide leadership decisions, enabling sales leaders to identify strengths, uncover weaknesses, and adjust strategies in real time.

Example: A sales leader tracks win rates to identify whether the team is effectively closing deals or if additional training in negotiation is required.

Motivating the Team

When shared transparently, metrics can motivate team members by showing progress toward goals and highlighting opportunities for improvement.

Example: A leaderboard displaying each salesperson's monthly performance fosters healthy competition and provides recognition for top performers.

Key Sales Metrics for Leadership

1. Revenue Metrics

- **Total Revenue:** Measures overall sales performance.
- **Revenue by Product/Service:** Highlights which offerings drive the most income.

> **Example:** A SaaS company notices that 60% of revenue comes from a specific product. The sales leader shifts focus to upselling additional services to these customers.

2. Sales Activity Metrics

- **Number of Calls/Emails:** Tracks outreach efforts.
- **Meetings Scheduled:** Evaluates lead engagement.

> **Example:** A sales rep making 20% fewer calls than peers is coached on time management and outreach strategies.

3. Conversion Metrics

- **Lead-to-Opportunity Rate:** Measures the percentage of leads that move to opportunities.
- **Opportunity-to-Close Rate (Win Rate):** Evaluates the effectiveness of closing strategies.

> **Example:** A sales team has a high lead-to-opportunity rate but a low win rate, indicating the need for better negotiation training.

4. Customer Metrics

- **Customer Lifetime Value (CLV):** Estimates the total revenue a customer will bring over their lifetime.
- **Customer Retention Rate:** Measures the percentage of customers retained over a specific period.

> **Example:** A high CLV but low retention rate suggests that initial sales strategies are strong, but post-sale engagement needs improvement.

5. Team Metrics

- **Quota Attainment:** Tracks how well individuals or teams meet their sales quotas.
- **Sales Cycle Length:** Measures the average time to close a deal.

Example: A sales team's average cycle length increases after a new product launch, prompting the sales leader to investigate bottlenecks in the sales process.

6. Profitability Metrics

- **Gross Margin by Sale:** Evaluates profitability per sale.
- **Cost of Sales:** Assesses the expense of closing deals.

Example: A company identifies that low-margin deals are consuming disproportionate resources, prompting a focus on higher-margin opportunities.

Using Metrics to Improve Performance

Benchmarking

Benchmarking against industry standards or historical data helps identify areas for improvement and set realistic goals.

Example: A team that closes deals at a 20% win rate compares this against the industry average of 30%, highlighting a need for better closing techniques.

Tracking Trends Over Time

Examining metrics over time allows leaders to spot trends and anticipate future challenges or opportunities.

Example: A steady decline in customer retention signals potential dissatisfaction, prompting an investigation into post-sale support.

Actionable Insights

Metrics should lead to actionable decisions. Data without context or follow-up can lead to misinterpretation and inaction.

Example: After identifying low quota attainment among new hires, a sales leader introduces an enhanced onboarding program.

Workshop
Activities

Activity 1: Designing a Sales Dashboard

Participants design a sales dashboard tailored to their organization's goals. They identify key metrics, determine how they will be visualized, and establish a cadence for reviews.

Activity 2: Analyzing Case Studies

Teams analyze case studies featuring hypothetical sales metrics, identify potential issues, and propose solutions to improve performance.

Activity 3: Metrics Role-Playing Exercise

Participants assume roles as sales reps and managers, discussing metrics during a one-on-one performance review. The activity emphasizes how to use metrics constructively to coach and motivate.

Conclusion

Measuring performance is a cornerstone of effective sales leadership. By focusing on the metrics that matter—such as revenue, conversion rates, customer retention, and profitability—leaders can make informed decisions that drive success. This chapter equips sales leaders with the tools to interpret and act on data, fostering a culture of continuous improvement and accountability within their teams.

CHAPTER 25

Feedback and Continuous Improvement: Establishing a Culture of Growth and Feedback

"

A culture of feedback fosters growth, innovation, and long-term excellence.

"

In a competitive sales environment, creating a culture of feedback and continuous improvement is essential for sustaining high performance and fostering personal and professional growth. This chapter explores how sales leaders can cultivate such a culture, emphasizing the value of feedback, techniques for effective communication, and strategies for integrating continuous improvement into daily operations.

The Importance of Feedback in Sales

Feedback as a Catalyst for Growth

Constructive feedback helps individuals recognize their strengths, identify areas for improvement, and develop new skills. It also reinforces desired behaviors and fosters a culture of accountability.

Example: A sales rep who receives specific feedback about improving their negotiation tactics may refine their approach, leading to higher close rates.

Feedback as a Two-Way Street

Feedback should not only flow from leaders to their teams but also from team members to leaders. This two-way exchange encourages trust, openness, and collaborative problem-solving.

Example: A sales team provides feedback to their manager about challenges in using a new CRM system, prompting the manager to arrange additional training.

Establishing a Culture of Feedback

1. Normalize Feedback

Feedback should be a regular part of the team's routine, not just limited to performance reviews. Frequent, informal feedback sessions reduce anxiety and make feedback more actionable.

> **Example:** A sales leader incorporates weekly "quick feedback" sessions where team members share successes and areas for improvement with each other.

2. Create a Safe Environment

Encourage open communication by fostering a judgment-free environment where employees feel comfortable giving and receiving feedback.

> **Example:** A sales leader emphasizes that feedback is about growth, not criticism, by highlighting examples of how constructive feedback has helped team members improve.

3. Be Specific and Actionable

Vague feedback can be demotivating. Leaders should provide specific examples and clear, actionable steps for improvement.

> **Example:** Instead of saying, *"You need to improve your closing skills,"* a manager says, *"In your last pitch, the client seemed uncertain. Next time, try using these closing techniques to address their hesitations."*

Techniques for Effective Feedback Delivery

The SBI Model (Situation-Behavior-Impact)

This model structures feedback by focusing on the specific situation, the observed behavior, and its impact. It minimizes ambiguity and makes feedback more meaningful.

> **Example:** *"During yesterday's client meeting (situation), you interrupted the client several times (behavior), which made them appear frustrated and less engaged (impact)."*

Balance Positive and Constructive Feedback

Start by recognizing achievements and then offer areas for improvement to ensure the feedback feels balanced and encouraging.

> **Example:** *"Your presentation was clear and engaging, but adding more data to support your arguments could make it even more convincing."*

Encourage Self-Reflection

Involve the individual in the feedback process by asking reflective questions, helping them take ownership of their growth.

> **Example:** *"How do you feel about your performance during that pitch? What do you think you could have done differently?"*

Continuous Improvement
Strategies

1. Encourage Ongoing Learning

Promote a mindset of continuous learning by providing access to resources such as training programs, webinars, and industry publications.

> **Example:** A sales team is encouraged to complete monthly online courses on advanced selling techniques, with rewards for consistent participation.

2. Use Metrics for Feedback

Leverage performance metrics to provide objective feedback and track progress over time.

> **Example:** A sales leader shares quarterly data on individual and team performance, highlighting improvements and areas that need attention.

3. Celebrate Small Wins

Recognizing incremental progress keeps the team motivated and reinforces the value of continuous improvement.

> **Example:** A sales rep who improves their win rate by 5% over a quarter is publicly recognized during a team meeting.

Workshop
Activities

Activity 1: Feedback Role-Playing

Participants practice giving and receiving feedback using real or hypothetical scenarios. Each role-play is followed by group discussion to evaluate effectiveness and areas for improvement.

Activity 2: Building a Feedback Framework

Teams collaborate to design a feedback framework for their sales department. They define the frequency, methods, and key principles of feedback to integrate into their culture.

Activity 3: Self-Reflection and Peer Feedback

Team members complete a self-assessment of their performance and exchange peer feedback in a structured session. This helps identify blind spots and build trust among team members.

Conclusion

Feedback and continuous improvement are fundamental to creating a high-performing sales team. By normalizing feedback, fostering a safe environment, and implementing structured improvement strategies, sales leaders can empower their teams to achieve their full potential. This chapter equips leaders with the tools to establish a culture of growth, ensuring long-term success for both individuals and the organization.

CHAPTER 26

Building a Legacy: Strategies for Leaving a Lasting Impact on Your Team and the Organization

> *The true mark of a leader is not what they achieve during their tenure, but the systems and culture they leave behind.*

A true measure of a leader's success lies not only in the results they achieve during their tenure but also in the lasting impact they leave behind. Building a legacy as a sales leader means creating systems, cultivating talent, and fostering a culture that thrives long after you've moved on. This chapter explores strategies for leaving a meaningful and enduring impact on your team and organization.

The Importance of Legacy Building

Legacy as Leadership

A strong legacy reflects leadership that transcends short-term gains, focusing instead on sustainable growth, team empowerment, and long-term organizational health.

■ **Example:** A sales leader who builds a scalable training program ensures that future teams can develop their skills, even in their absence.

Inspiring Loyalty and Growth

Leaving a legacy fosters loyalty among your team members and instills a sense of pride in contributing to something greater than themselves.

■ **Example:** A leader who creates a culture of transparency and recognition leaves behind a team that values collaboration and mutual respect.

Strategies for Building a Legacy

1. Develop Future Leaders

Empowering and mentoring future leaders ensures that the organization will continue to thrive with strong leadership in place.

■ **Example:** Identify high-potential team members and provide them with leadership opportunities, such as leading special projects or acting as team leads during major initiatives.

2. Build Scalable Systems

Create processes and tools that streamline operations and can adapt to future challenges, ensuring continuity and efficiency.

Example: Design a sales playbook that outlines best practices, workflows, and customer engagement strategies, providing a reference for future sales teams.

3. Foster a Culture of Excellence

Creating a positive, high-performing culture is one of the most enduring contributions a leader can make. This includes emphasizing core values, such as integrity, collaboration, and innovation.

Example: Establish regular team-building events and recognition programs to strengthen team cohesion and commitment to shared goals.

4. Document Institutional Knowledge

Preserving institutional knowledge helps ensure that valuable lessons and strategies are not lost during transitions.

Example: Maintain a repository of case studies, client success stories, and team performance data that can guide future decision-making.

5. Prioritize Long-Term Relationships

Cultivate strong relationships with clients, partners, and stakeholders that can endure beyond your tenure.

■ **Example:** Develop a client relationship strategy that emphasizes consistency and trust, ensuring that key accounts remain loyal to the organization.

Examples of Enduring Legacies

Case Study 1: Creating a Training Academy

A sales leader in the retail industry launched an internal training academy to onboard and develop new sales reps. This academy continued to operate successfully after the leader's departure, maintaining high training standards and contributing to the company's success.

Case Study 2: Building a Recognition Culture

At a tech company, a sales leader implemented an employee recognition platform where peers could celebrate one another's achievements. The initiative boosted morale and remained a staple of the company culture long after the leader moved on.

Workshop
Activities

Activity 1: Legacy Vision Exercise

Participants reflect on the question: "What do I want my leadership legacy to be?" They write down their vision and discuss it with peers, exploring ways to translate their ideas into actionable plans.

Activity 2: Identifying Long-Term Opportunities

Teams brainstorm initiatives that could have a lasting impact on their organization, such as process improvements, mentorship programs, or client retention strategies. They then create a roadmap for implementing these ideas.

Activity 3: Building a Knowledge Repository

Participants collaborate to design a structure for preserving institutional knowledge, such as creating a shared online library of resources, best practices, and sales templates.

Conclusion

Building a legacy requires intentionality, vision, and a focus on creating systems and cultures that outlast your tenure. By developing future leaders, implementing scalable solutions, fostering a culture of excellence, and documenting institutional knowledge, sales leaders can leave an indelible mark on their teams and organizations. This chapter equips leaders with actionable strategies to build a legacy that will inspire growth and success for years to come.

The Future of Sales Leadership: Preparing for New Challenges and Opportunities in Sales

"

Tomorrow's leaders will thrive by embracing change, leveraging technology, and leading with empathy and vision.

"

The sales landscape is constantly evolving, driven by technological advancements, shifting buyer behaviors, and changes in global markets. Sales leaders must adapt to these changes while preparing their teams to thrive in an uncertain and dynamic future. This chapter explores emerging trends, potential challenges, and new opportunities in sales, equipping leaders with strategies to stay ahead of the curve.

Emerging Trends in Sales Leadership

1. The Rise of AI and Automation

Artificial intelligence (AI) and automation are revolutionizing sales processes by streamlining workflows, personalizing customer interactions, and providing data-driven insights.

Example: AI-powered tools like chatbots handle initial customer inquiries, while predictive analytics help sales teams identify high-priority leads based on historical data.

2. Data-Driven Decision Making

Access to advanced analytics enables sales leaders to make informed decisions, track performance in real-time, and identify areas for improvement.

Example: A sales leader uses customer data to identify declining engagement rates and launches targeted campaigns to re-engage dormant accounts.

3. Virtual and Hybrid Selling

The shift to virtual and hybrid selling models has made remote communication and digital sales platforms essential. These approaches allow sales teams to reach wider audiences while maintaining personalized connections.

Example: A global software company implements virtual demos and webinars to engage prospects across multiple time zones, reducing the need for costly in-person meetings.

4. Emphasis on Customer Experience

Buyers increasingly value seamless and personalized experiences over transactional sales. This requires sales leaders to align their strategies with customer-centric principles.

■ **Example:** A retail brand integrates customer feedback loops into its sales process, ensuring that reps address pain points and tailor solutions to individual needs.

Challenges in the Future of Sales

1. Talent Acquisition and Retention

Finding and retaining top sales talent will become more challenging as job markets grow increasingly competitive. Leaders must focus on creating a compelling employer value proposition (EVP).

■ **Example:** A company enhances its EVP by offering robust career development programs, competitive compensation, and a supportive workplace culture.

2. Managing Remote Teams

Leading geographically dispersed teams requires a new approach to communication, collaboration, and motivation.

■ **Example:** A sales leader schedules weekly virtual check-ins and implements cloud-based tools for seamless collaboration among remote team members.

3. Adapting to Rapid Market Changes

Economic uncertainty and market disruptions demand that sales leaders remain agile and responsive to change.

Example: A sales leader in the travel industry rapidly pivots to promoting local experiences when international travel is restricted, ensuring the team continues to meet targets.

Opportunities for Sales Leaders

1. Leveraging Technology for Competitive Advantage

Sales leaders who embrace emerging technologies can gain a competitive edge by improving efficiency and customer engagement.

Example: A sales team uses augmented reality (AR) tools to provide immersive product demonstrations, setting themselves apart from competitors.

2. Expanding into New Markets

Globalization and advancements in communication technology present opportunities to tap into previously inaccessible markets.

Example: A SaaS company expands into emerging markets by tailoring its sales strategy to local languages, cultures, and business practices.

3. Prioritizing Diversity and Inclusion

Building diverse and inclusive sales teams enhances creativity, decision-making, and customer understanding.

> **Example:** A sales leader implements a diversity hiring initiative and fosters an inclusive culture through team-building workshops and open dialogues.

Preparing for the Future

Upskilling and Reskilling Teams

Continual learning is essential for keeping teams competitive. Sales leaders must invest in training programs that address both technical and soft skills.

> **Example:** A sales team participates in workshops on AI tools, advanced negotiation techniques, and emotional intelligence to enhance their adaptability and effectiveness.

Adopting Agile Leadership

Agile leadership involves flexibility, quick decision-making, and a focus on collaboration. This approach helps leaders navigate uncertainty and drive innovation.

> **Example:** During a sudden shift in customer preferences, an agile sales leader convenes a cross-functional task force to devise and implement a new sales strategy within weeks.

Workshop Activities

Activity 1: Trend Analysis and Strategic Planning

Participants research emerging trends in sales and create strategic plans to address them. Teams present their plans, focusing on how to integrate new technologies or adapt to changing customer needs.

Activity 2: Building a Future-Ready Team

Participants assess the skills required for future sales success and design a training roadmap for their teams, including technical, analytical, and interpersonal skills.

Activity 3: Scenario Planning

Teams develop responses to hypothetical future challenges, such as a major market disruption or the emergence of a new competitor, emphasizing agility and innovation.

Conclusion

The future of sales leadership will be defined by adaptability, innovation, and a commitment to continuous learning. By embracing emerging technologies, addressing new challenges, and capitalizing on opportunities, sales leaders can prepare their teams to thrive in an ever-changing landscape. This chapter provides a roadmap for future-ready leadership, ensuring long-term success in a dynamic sales environment.

PRACTICAL TOOLS AND RESOURCES FOR SALES LEADERS

LEADERSHIP CHECKLISTS: DAILY HABITS FOR SALES LEADERS

Effective sales leadership isn't just about big-picture strategy or quarterly results—it's about mastering the habits and routines that drive daily performance and long-term success. By breaking your responsibilities into manageable tasks and adhering to consistent routines, you can ensure your team stays motivated, aligned, and productive. This section provides a comprehensive checklist of daily, weekly, and monthly habits, along with practical time management tips and real-world examples of how top-performing leaders structure their day.

Daily Leadership Checklist

Your daily actions set the tone for your team and ensure alignment with broader goals. Focus on habits that build trust, provide support, and keep momentum strong.

1. Morning Prioritization

- Review your team's metrics from the previous day (e.g., calls made, deals closed, pipeline activity).
- Identify critical issues or opportunities requiring immediate attention.
- Set your top three priorities for the day.

2. One-on-One Check-Ins

- Spend 10–15 minutes with individual team members to address roadblocks, provide encouragement, or offer quick coaching.
- **Tip:** Use these sessions to align their efforts with team objectives.

3. Communicate with the Team

- Share updates, motivational messages, or insights through email, chat, or a quick stand-up meeting.
- Ensure your team feels informed and connected to the broader organizational goals.

4. Coaching in Real Time

- Listen to live calls or shadow meetings to provide actionable feedback.
- Praise what's working well and suggest specific improvements.

5. End-of-Day Reflection

- Review your progress on the day's priorities.
- Acknowledge successes and note unresolved issues to address the following day.

Weekly Leadership Checklist

Weekly habits focus on maintaining team alignment, addressing bigger-picture issues, and fostering collaboration.

1. Weekly Team Meetings

- Host a structured meeting to review performance, share updates, and discuss upcoming goals.
- Include time for team members to share wins, challenges, and best practices.
- Example Agenda:
  - » **10 minutes:** Key metrics review
  - » **15 minutes:** Team shout-outs and lessons learned
  - » **15 minutes:** Upcoming goals and action items

2. Pipeline Reviews

- Analyze the team's sales pipeline to identify stalled deals or areas requiring extra focus.
- Collaborate with your team to develop strategies for high-priority opportunities.

3. Training or Skill Development

- Dedicate time each week for team training sessions or workshops.

- Focus on areas such as objection handling, product updates, or negotiation tactics.

4. Peer Collaboration

Encourage collaboration across departments, such as marketing or customer success, to improve lead quality or post-sale handoffs.

Monthly Leadership Checklist

Monthly habits allow you to focus on strategic planning, long-term development, and deeper team engagement.

1. Strategy Reviews

- Evaluate the effectiveness of current sales strategies and adjust based on performance data or market trends.
- Involve your team in brainstorming sessions to generate ideas for improvement.

2. Individual Development Plans

- Meet with each team member to review their performance against personal goals and identify growth opportunities.
- **Tip:** Tailor these conversations to their unique strengths and challenges.

3. Celebrate Milestones

- Recognize team and individual achievements, such as surpassing targets or landing key accounts.
- Use both public recognition (e.g., team meetings) and private appreciation (e.g., personalized notes).

4. Budget and Resource Planning

- Review your team's resource needs, such as tools, technology, or additional personnel.
- Ensure alignment with organizational budgets and sales targets.

Time Management
Tips for Sales Leaders

Balancing strategic planning with team support can be challenging, but with intentional time management, you can achieve both.

1. Block Your Time

- Allocate specific blocks of time for coaching, strategy, and administrative tasks.
- Example:
  - » **8:30–9:00 AM** : Morning prioritization
  - » **10:00–11:00 AM** : One-on-one check-ins
  - » **1:00–2:00 PM** : Strategy work
  - » **4:30–5:00 PM** : End-of-day reflection

2. Delegate Where Possible

Empower team members to take ownership of tasks like reporting or meeting preparation, freeing you to focus on higher-level priorities.

3. Protect Time for Deep Work

Dedicate at least one hour per day to uninterrupted strategic thinking or problem-solving.

4. Leverage Technology

Use tools like CRM dashboards, calendar apps, and project management software to stay organized and save time.

A Day in the Life of
a Top-Performing
Sales Leader

Here's an example of how a high-performing sales manager structures their day for maximum impact:

8:30 AM	Review team performance metrics and set priorities.
9:00 AM	Morning team huddle to share updates and align on goals.
10:00 AM	One-on-one coaching sessions with three team members.
12:00 PM	Lunch and catch-up on industry news or professional development.
1:00 PM	Listen to live sales calls and provide real-time feedback.
3:00 PM	Pipeline review and strategy brainstorming with senior reps.
4:30 PM	Send an end-of-day email highlighting team wins and progress.
5:00 PM	Reflect on the day's successes and prepare for tomorrow.

SELF-REFLECTION TOOLKIT FOR LEADERS

Great leadership starts with self-awareness. The best leaders take the time to reflect on their strengths, challenges, and opportunities for growth, using introspection as a foundation for continuous improvement. This section provides tools to encourage regular self-reflection, including journaling prompts, a leadership self-assessment quiz, and actionable tips for setting personal growth goals. By committing to self-reflection, you can evolve as a leader and better serve your team.

Journaling Prompts
for Leadership Growth

Journaling is a powerful way to process experiences, gain clarity, and identify areas for improvement. Use the following prompts to reflect on your leadership journey:

1. Reflecting on Successes

- What is a recent success I'm particularly proud of as a leader?
- What actions or decisions contributed to that success?
- How did this success impact my team, organization, or clients?

2. Analyzing Challenges

- What leadership challenge have I faced recently, and how did I handle it?
- What did I learn from this experience, and what would I do differently next time?
- Did I involve the right people to address the challenge effectively?

3. Identifying Opportunities

- What areas of my leadership could I improve to better serve my team?
- Are there new skills or knowledge I need to acquire to stay ahead in my role?
- What feedback have I received recently that I could act on?

4. Focusing on Team Dynamics

- How well do I understand my team's individual strengths, motivations, and challenges?
- What steps can I take to build stronger relationships with my team members?
- How have I contributed to fostering a positive team culture?

5. Vision and Strategy

- How aligned is my team with our vision and goals?
- Are the strategies I've implemented delivering the desired results?
- What changes or innovations could I introduce to drive greater success?

Leadership Self-Assessment Quiz

This self-assessment quiz helps you evaluate key aspects of your leadership, from emotional intelligence to communication effectiveness. Rate yourself on a scale from 1 (needs improvement) to 5 (excellent).

1. Emotional Intelligence

- I am aware of my emotions and how they affect my behavior.
- I can manage stress and remain calm under pressure.
- I empathize with my team members and understand their perspectives.

2. Communication Skills

- I communicate my vision and goals clearly and effectively.

- I actively listen to my team and encourage open dialogue.
- I handle difficult conversations with tact and professionalism.

3. Decision-Making

- I make timely, informed decisions based on data and intuition.
- I involve others in decision-making when appropriate.
- I evaluate the potential risks and benefits of my decisions.

4. Team Leadership

- I provide my team with the resources and support they need to succeed.
- I regularly recognize and celebrate team and individual accomplishments.
- I effectively address underperformance and resolve conflicts.

5. Adaptability and Growth

- I embrace change and help my team adapt to new circumstances.
- I seek feedback to improve my leadership skills.
- I am committed to learning and growing as a leader.

Scoring and Reflection:

- Total your score for each category and identify areas with lower ratings.
- Use this insight to pinpoint areas for improvement and prioritize your development efforts.

Tips for Setting Personal Growth Goals

Once you've reflected on your leadership journey and assessed your skills, the next step is setting actionable goals for self-improvement. Use these tips to create effective personal growth goals:

1. Align Goals with Your Leadership Role

Identify areas of growth that will have the greatest impact on your team and organization.

■ **Example:** If your team struggles with communication, set a goal to improve your active listening skills and facilitate better team discussions.

2. Use the SMART Framework

Create goals that are Specific, Measurable, Achievable, Relevant, and Time-bound.

■ **Example:** "Attend two leadership workshops on emotional intelligence within the next three months."

3. Balance Strengths and Weaknesses

Build on your strengths while addressing areas that need improvement.

■ **Example:** If you excel at strategic planning but struggle with delegation, focus on developing trust in your team and empowering them to take ownership.

4. Track Progress and Reflect Regularly

Schedule time each month to review your progress toward your goals and make adjustments as needed.

Example: Keep a journal of specific actions you've taken to improve, along with their outcomes.

5. Seek Feedback and Mentorship

Ask trusted colleagues or mentors for feedback on your progress. Their insights can provide valuable perspectives and help you stay accountable.

QUICK-REFERENCE GUIDE TO MOTIVATING YOUR TEAM

Motivation is the lifeblood of any successful sales team. As a leader, it's your role to keep morale high and performance consistent, even in challenging times. While long-term strategies are important, having quick and effective motivation techniques at your disposal can make a big difference in day-to-day team dynamics. This cheat sheet provides 10 actionable techniques, tips for identifying individual motivators, and guidance on avoiding burnout while driving results.

10 Quick Motivation Techniques

1. Public Recognition

Acknowledge achievements in team meetings, newsletters, or group chats.

◾ **Example:** *"Let's all give Sarah a round of applause for closing the biggest deal of the quarter!"*

2. Personalized Incentives

Reward team members with incentives tailored to their preferences, such as gift cards, extra time off, or experiences.

◾ **Example:** A high performer might appreciate a dinner voucher at their favorite restaurant.

3. Team Challenges

Organize friendly competitions with small rewards for achieving specific goals, like most new leads generated in a week.

◾ **Example:** *"The winner of this week's challenge gets an extra day off!"*

4. Shout-Out Boards

Create a physical or digital board where team members can recognize each other's contributions.

◾ **Example:** A Slack channel where peers can post shout-outs for collaboration or creative solutions.

5. Surprise Perks

Surprise your team with small, thoughtful gestures, like catered lunches or afternoon coffee runs.

■ **Example:** *"You've been working hard this week—pizza's on me today!"*

6. Development Opportunities

Offer opportunities for personal and professional growth, such as training sessions, certifications, or leadership workshops.

■ **Example:** *"We've partnered with a top sales coach for a workshop next month—let's elevate our skills!"*

7. Collaborative Goal-Setting

Involve your team in setting sales goals and planning how to achieve them.

■ **Example:** *"Let's brainstorm together how we can hit a 10% increase in revenue this quarter."*

8. Flexibility Rewards

Allow team members to adjust their schedules or work remotely as a reward for meeting milestones.

■ **Example:** *"You've hit your targets early—why not take Friday off?"*

9. Celebrate Milestones

Recognize birthdays, work anniversaries, and personal

milestones to make team members feel valued.

> **Example:** *"Happy 2-year anniversary with the team, John! We appreciate everything you've done."*

10. Lead by Example

Show enthusiasm and commitment in your own work to inspire your team.

> **Example:** Join your team in a sales challenge or take time to personally coach someone struggling.

Tips for Identifying What Motivates Each Individual

Not everyone is motivated by the same factors. Understanding individual drivers can help you tailor your approach to each team member.

1. Ask Directly

During one-on-one meetings, ask team members what motivates them and what rewards they value most.

> **Example Questions:** *"What makes you feel most appreciated at work?"* or *"What would make hitting your targets feel extra rewarding?"*

2. Observe Behavior

Pay attention to how individuals react to different types of recognition, challenges, or incentives.

- **Example:** If someone lights up when praised publicly, use that to keep them engaged.

3. Review Past Performance

Analyze what initiatives or rewards led to spikes in performance for each person.

- **Example:** A team member who thrived in a competition may be driven by challenges.

4. Consider Personality Types

Use personality assessments (e.g., DISC, MBTI) to understand intrinsic motivators and tailor your strategies accordingly.

- **Example:** An analytical team member may value data-driven feedback, while a creative one may appreciate freedom in their approach.

CRISIS LEADERSHIP PLAYBOOK

Crisis leadership is a defining test of any sales leader's ability to remain calm, decisive, and resilient under pressure. Whether facing sudden market disruptions, internal organizational shifts, or global economic challenges, your response sets the tone for your team's performance and morale. This playbook provides actionable steps for effective communication, task prioritization, and resource reallocation during a crisis, along with real-world examples of sales leaders who turned challenges into opportunities.

Steps to Communicate
Effectively During a Crisis

Clear, timely, and empathetic communication is crucial in navigating uncertainty. Here's how to ensure your messaging keeps your team informed and focused:

1. Acknowledge the Crisis Immediately

Avoid delays in addressing the situation. Transparency fosters trust and prevents speculation.

Example: *"We've seen a sudden dip in our market due to new competitor pricing. Here's what we know so far and what we're doing about it."*

2. Provide Regular Updates

- Maintain a steady flow of information, even if there's little new to report. Uncertainty is reduced when your team knows you're actively monitoring the situation.
- **Tip:** Schedule daily or weekly briefings to keep everyone aligned.

3. Be Honest but Optimistic

Share the reality of the challenge while emphasizing your confidence in the team's ability to overcome it.

Example: *"Yes, this is a tough quarter, but we've faced challenges before, and I believe we'll come out stronger."*

4. Listen and Respond to Concerns

Create opportunities for team members to share their fears and questions, either in one-on-ones or team meetings.

■ **Example:** *"I know many of you are worried about how this will affect our goals. Let's talk through your concerns and address them together."*

5. Clarify Action Plans

Break down your strategy into actionable steps, so your team knows exactly what to focus on.

■ **Example:** *"Our immediate priorities are retaining key clients, accelerating prospecting efforts, and re-evaluating our pricing strategy."*

Frameworks for Prioritizing Tasks and Reallocating Resources

In a crisis, it's essential to act swiftly and decisively. Use these frameworks to focus on what matters most and deploy your resources effectively.

1. The 3-Priority Rule

Simplify your team's focus by identifying the top three priorities that will have the biggest impact during the crisis.

■ **Example:**
  • **Priority 1:** Retain existing customers by enhancing

service and offering flexible terms.

- **Priority 2:** Accelerate efforts to close high-probability deals in the pipeline.

- **Priority 3:** Pause lower-priority projects to free up time and resources.

2. The ABC Resource Allocation Framework

Categorize tasks and resources into three groups to ensure optimal deployment:

A. **Essential Tasks:** Activities that directly address the crisis (e.g., client retention, high-priority deal closures).

B. **Supportive Tasks:** Secondary activities that aid the essentials (e.g., marketing support, training).

C. **Deferred Tasks:** Non-critical activities that can be paused or rescheduled (e.g., new product launches, long-term projects).

3. The Crisis Response Checklist

Use this checklist to ensure nothing falls through the cracks:

- **Assess:** Evaluate the immediate impact of the crisis on sales goals, clients, and team dynamics.

- **Plan:** Develop a clear response strategy with input from key stakeholders.

- **Act:** Execute the plan with urgency, ensuring alignment across all team members.

- **Monitor:** Track results daily and adjust the strategy as new information emerges.

- **Review:** Conduct a post-crisis review to document lessons learned and improve future responses.

Real-World Examples of
Sales Leaders Navigating Crises

Example 1: Pivoting During a Market Downturn

When a mid-sized logistics company faced a sudden market downturn due to increased fuel costs, the sales leader quickly shifted priorities. They focused the team's efforts on securing long-term contracts with existing clients, offering locked-in pricing to mitigate risk. By reallocating resources to client retention and upselling additional services, the company weathered the downturn and even increased client loyalty.

Example 2: Adapting to Remote Sales During the Pandemic

At the onset of COVID-19, a SaaS company's sales team struggled to adjust to remote selling. The sales director immediately invested in virtual training for the team, implemented video conferencing tools, and redesigned presentations for virtual delivery. The swift adaptation not only helped the team meet their goals but also expanded their reach to international markets.

Example 3: Managing Team Morale Amid Layoffs

When a retail company underwent layoffs, the sales manager focused on maintaining morale among the remaining team members. They held weekly town halls to provide updates, launched a peer-recognition program to boost engagement, and worked closely with HR to ensure transparent communication. Despite the challenges, the team rallied to exceed their quarterly targets.

ELEVATING SALES LEADERSHIP FOR A DYNAMIC FUTURE

Sales leadership is both an art and a science—an evolving discipline that requires adaptability, empathy, strategy, and vision. Throughout this book, we have explored the multifaceted nature of sales leadership, from setting the foundation with a compelling vision and building high-performing teams to navigating change, fostering growth, and preparing for the future.

The role of a sales leader extends beyond meeting quarterly targets or closing deals. It is about inspiring teams, cultivating talent, and creating an environment where innovation and resilience thrive. Great leaders leave behind more than just successful numbers; they leave a legacy of empowered individuals, scalable systems, and a culture of excellence that endures.

As the world of sales becomes more complex with advancements in technology, shifting customer behaviors, and global challenges, the role of a sales leader has never been more critical—or more exciting. The strategies, tools, and insights shared in this book are designed to equip you with the skills needed to navigate these complexities and elevate your leadership impact.

Key Takeaways

1. **Vision and Strategy Matter:** Effective leaders craft clear visions and align their strategies to inspire and drive their teams toward shared goals.

2. **People Are the Priority:** From nurturing rising stars to addressing challenging personalities, leadership begins with understanding and valuing the human element.

3. **Data and Technology Empower Leadership:** Leveraging metrics, analytics, and cutting-edge tools enables leaders to make informed decisions and remain agile in a competitive market.

4. **Change is Constant:** Whether navigating new market dynamics or leading through organizational shifts, the ability to adapt is a hallmark of successful leadership.

5. **Leave a Legacy:** True leadership transcends personal achievements, creating lasting systems, cultures, and opportunities for future leaders to flourish.

A Call to Action

Leadership is a journey, not a destination. As you reflect on the insights from this book, consider how you will apply them to your unique leadership context. What legacy do you want to leave? How will you inspire and empower your team to achieve more than they thought possible?

By committing to continuous improvement, embracing challenges as opportunities, and leading with integrity, you have the power to transform not only your team but also your organization and industry. The future of sales leadership is in your hands—make it bold, innovative, and inspiring.

Thank you for taking this journey through Elevate: Mastering the Art of Sales Leadership. Now, go forward and lead with purpose.

APPENDIX: FURTHER READING BY CHAPTER TOPICS

Chapter 1. The Role of a Sales Leader: Understanding Your Impact on the Team and the Business

- *"The Sales Manager's Handbook"* by **Jonathan Whistman** (2016)

- *"Drive: The Surprising Truth About What Motivates Us"* by **Daniel H. Pink** (2009)

- *"Sales Leadership: The Essential Leadership Framework to Coach Sales Champions, Inspire Excellence, and Exceed Your Business Goals"* by **Keith Rosen** (2018)

Chapter 2. Leadership vs. Management: Identifying the Differences and When to Apply Each Skill

- *"Leaders Eat Last"* by **Simon Sinek** (2014)

- *"Management vs. Leadership: A Practical Guide"* by **Morgen Witzel** (2017)

- *"The Making of a Manager: What to Do When Everyone Looks to You"* by **Julie Zhuo** (2019)

Chapter 3. Setting the Vision: Crafting and Communicating a Compelling Sales Vision

- *"Start with Why: How Great Leaders Inspire Everyone to Take Action"* by **Simon Sinek** (2009)

- *"Measure What Matters"* by **John Doerr** (2018)

- *"Visionary Leadership in a Turbulent World"* by **Joan Marques** (2020)

Chapter 4. Building Your Team: Hiring the Right People

and Positioning Them for Success

- *"Who: The A Method for Hiring"* by **Geoff Smart and Randy Street** (2008)

- *"It's the Manager"* by **Jim Clifton and Jim Harter** (2019)

- *"Work Rules!: Insights from Inside Google That Will Transform How You Live and Lead"* by **Laszlo Bock** (2015)

Chapter 5. Emotional Intelligence: Harnessing EQ to Lead and Inspire Your Team

- *"Emotional Intelligence 2.0"* by **Travis Bradberry and Jean Greaves** (2009)

- *"Primal Leadership: Unleashing the Power of Emotional Intelligence"* by **Daniel Goleman, Richard Boyatzis, and Annie McKee** (2002)

- *"Emotional Intelligence for the Modern Leader: A Guide to Cultivating Effective Leadership and Organizations"* by **Christopher D. Connors** (2020)

Chaper 6. Communication Mastery: Effective Communication Strategies for Sales Leaders

- *"Crucial Conversations: Tools for Talking When Stakes Are High"* by **Kerry Patterson, Joseph Grenny, and others** (2002)

- *"Fierce Conversations"* by **Susan Scott** (2002)

- *"Communicate with Mastery: Speak with Confidence and Write for Impact"* by **JD Schramm and Kara Levy** (2020)

Chapter 7. Decision Making: Techniques for Making Quick and Effective Decisions Under Pressure

- *"Thinking, Fast and Slow"* by **Daniel Kahneman** (2011)

- *"Decisive: How to Make Better Choices in Life and Work"* by

Chip Heath and Dan Heath (2013)

- *"Smart Leadership: Four Simple Choices to Scale Your Impact"* by **Mark Miller** (2022)

Chapter 8. Conflict Resolution: Handling Disputes and Maintaining Team Harmony

- *"Getting to Yes: Negotiating Agreement Without Giving In"* by **Roger Fisher, William Ury, and Bruce Patton** (1981)
- *"Difficult Conversations: How to Discuss What Matters Most"* by **Douglas Stone, Bruce Patton, and Sheila Heen** (1999)
- *"Conflict Without Casualties: A Field Guide for Leading with Compassionate Accountability"* by **Nate Regier** (2017)

Chapter 9. Designing Sales Strategies: Creating Plans That Deliver Results

- *"The Challenger Sale: Taking Control of the Customer Conversation"* by **Matthew Dixon and Brent Adamson** (2011)
- *"SPIN Selling"* by **Neil Rackham** (1988)
- *"Sales Management That Works: How to Sell in a World That Never Stops Changing"* by **Frank V. Cespedes** (2021)

Chapter 10. Market Analysis and Adaptation: Understanding and Reacting to Market Dynamics

- *"Blue Ocean Strategy"* by **W. Chan Kim and Renée Mauborgne** (2005)
- *"Competing on Analytics"* by **Thomas H. Davenport and Jeanne G. Harris** (2007)
- *"Rethinking Competitive Advantage: New Rules for the Digital Age"* by **Ram Charan** (2021)

Chapter 11. Operational Efficiency: Streamlining Processes for Maximum Productivity

- *"The Lean Startup"* by **Eric Ries** (2011)
- *"Work the System: The Simple Mechanics of Making More and Working Less"* by **Sam Carpenter** (2008)
- *"The Art of Efficiency: Tools and Insights for Optimizing Performance"* by **Daniel Espy** (2022)

Chapter 12. Technology in Sales: Leveraging Tools for Enhanced Performance

- *"AI for Sales: How Artificial Intelligence Is Changing Sales"* by **Chad Burmeister** (2020)
- *"Salesforce For Dummies"* by **Tom Wong and Liz Kao** (2016)
- *"Tech-Powered Sales: Achieve Superhuman Sales Skills"* by **Justin Michael and Tony Hughes** (2021)

Chapter 13. Coaching and Mentoring: Developing Your Team Through Continuous Learning

- *"The Coaching Habit"* by **Michael Bungay Stanier** (2016)
- *"Multipliers: How the Best Leaders Make Everyone Smarter"* by **Liz Wiseman** (2010)
- *"Coaching Salespeople into Sales Champions: A Tactical Playbook for Managers and Executives"* by **Keith Rosen** (2018)

Chapter 14. Motivational Techniques: Strategies to Inspire and Drive Your Team to Exceed Targets

- *"Drive: The Surprising Truth About What Motivates Us"* by **Daniel H. Pink** (2009)
- *"The Carrot Principle"* by **Adrian Gostick and Chester Elton** (2009)

- *"Motivate People: Inspire Excellence in Your Team"* by **Aimee Bernstein** (2020)

Chapter 15. Designing Effective Sales Compensation Plans: Aligning Incentives with Goals

- *"Compensating the Sales Force"* by **David J. Cichelli** (2010)
- *"Sales Compensation Essentials"* by **David J. Cichelli** (2004)
- *"Sales Compensation Made Simple: How to Design a Plan that Works"* by **David W. Cichelli** (2022)

Chapter 16. Change Management: Leading Your Team Through Shifts in Strategy and Market Conditions

- *"Leading Change"* by **John P. Kotter** (1996)
- *"Switch: How to Change Things When Change Is Hard"* by **Chip Heath and Dan Heath** (2010)
- *"Beyond Digital: How Great Leaders Transform Their Organizations and Shape the Future"* by **Paul Leinwand and Mahadeva Matt Mani** (2022)

Chapter 17. Customer Relationship Leadership: Cultivating Key Relationships for Long-Term Success

- *"The Trusted Advisor"* by **David H. Maister, Charles H. Green, and Robert M. Galford** (2000)
- *"Customer Success"* by **Nick Mehta, Dan Steinman, and Lincoln Murphy** (2016)
- *"The Customer-Driven Culture: A Microsoft Story"* by **Travis Lowdermilk and Monty Hammontree** (2021)

Chapter 18. Identifying Problematic Behavior

- *"Radical Candor: Be a Kick-Ass Boss Without Losing Your*

Humanity" by **Kim Scott** (2017)

- *"Crucial Accountability"* by **Kerry Patterson and Joseph Grenny** (2013)

- *"No Hard Feelings: The Secret Power of Embracing Emotions at Work"* by **Liz Fosslien and Mollie West Duffy** (2019)

Chapter 19. Effective Remediation Strategies

- *"First, Break All the Rules"* by **Marcus Buckingham and Curt Coffman** (1999)

- *"The Five Dysfunctions of a Team"* by **Patrick Lencioni** (2002)

- *"How to Be a Great Boss"* by **Gino Wickman and René Boer** (2016)

Chapter 20. Legal and Ethical Considerations

- *"Employment Law for Business"* by **Dawn D. Bennett-Alexander and Laura P. Hartman** (2018)

- *"Business Ethics: Ethical Decision Making & Cases"* by **O.C. Ferrell, John Fraedrich, and Linda Ferrell** (2018)

- *"HR on Purpose!!: Developing Deliberate People Passion"* by **Steve Browne** (2017)

Chapter 21. Discovering Hidden Talent

- *"StrengthsFinder 2.0"* by **Tom Rath** (2007)

- *"The Talent Code"* by **Daniel Coyle** (2009)

- *"The Talent Manifesto: How Disrupting People Strategies Maximizes Business Results"* by **RJ Heckman** (2018)

Chapter 22. Developing Emerging Leaders

- *"Leaders Made Here: Building a Leadership Culture"* by **Mark Miller** (2016)

- *"Your Leadership Pipeline"* by **Ram Charan, Stephen Drotter, and James Noel** (2000)
- *"The Emerging Leader: Prepare Your Team for Leadership Success"* by **Sean O'Brien** (2021)

Chapter 23. Balancing Focus

- *"Managing the One-Minute Manager"* by **Ken Blanchard** (2015)
- *"The Coaching Effect"* by **Bill Eckstrom and Sarah Wirth** (2019)
- *"Radical Focus: Achieving Your Most Important Goals with Objectives and Key Results"* by **Christina Wodtke** (2016)

Chapter 24. Measuring Performance

- *"Sales Analytics: Strategy, Planning, and Management"* by **Andris A. Zoltners, Prabhakant Sinha, and Sally E. Lorimer** (2014)
- *"Key Performance Indicators (KPI): Developing, Implementing, and Using Winning KPIs"* by **David Parmenter** (2015)
- *"Measure Up: Mastering Performance Metrics"* by **Mike Bourne and Pippa Bourne** (2018)

Chapter 25. Feedback and Continuous Improvement

- *"Thanks for the Feedback: The Science and Art of Receiving Feedback Well"* by **Douglas Stone and Sheila Heen** (2014)
- *"Let's Talk: Make Effective Feedback Your Superpower"* by **Therese Huston** (2021)

Chapter 26. Building a Legacy

- *"Your Leadership Legacy: Why Looking Toward the Future Will Make You a Better Leader Today"* by **Marta Brooks,**

Julie Stark, and Sarah Caverhill (2006)

- *"Leaders Made Here"* by **Mark Miller** (2016)
- *"Legacy in the Making: Building a Long-Term Brand to Stand Out in a Short-Term World"* by **Mark Miller and Lucas Conley** (2018)

Chapter 27. The Future of Sales Leadership

- *"The Future of Selling: The Essential Guide to B2B Sales"* by **John Smibert, Wayne Moloney, and Jeff Clulow** (2020)
- *"AI Superpowers: China, Silicon Valley, and the New World Order"* by **Kai-Fu Lee** (2018)
- *"The Future Leader: 9 Skills and Mindsets to Succeed in the Next Decade"* by **Jacob Morgan** (2020)

Thank you for reading,
and here's to your ongoing success!

About The Author

Mort Greenberg brings over 25 years of experience as a business leader, working with tech start-ups and major media companies. Rising from an Account Executive to the President of a division with 800+ employees generating $220 million in annual revenue, Mort has supported revenue efforts for various companies as they navigated the need for growth, mergers, acquisitions, and IPOs. He was instrumental in shaping the digital advertising landscape during the early days of the Internet at Excite.com and Ask Jeeves. He has also held leadership roles at IAC / InterActiveCorp, NBC Universal, Nokia, and iHeartMedia. Along the way, he launched two companies of his own, FitAd and MindFlight, and learned that start-ups are not always successful. Since 2016, he has been helping turn around distressed media properties into profitable companies for a global private equity firm. The #1 lesson he has learned in all his years is that by improving people's revenue mindset, business problems are healed, and teams are motivated through innovation that new revenue affords.

www.ingramcontent.com/pod-product-compliance
Lightning Source LLC
Chambersburg PA
CBHW040852210326
41597CB00029B/4821